LEARN TRUFFLE

100+ Coding Q&A

Yasin Cakal

Code of Code

CONTENTS

INTRODUCTION

Welcome to "Learn Truffle", the ultimate book for becoming a proficient Blockchain developer using Truffle! Truffle is a popular development framework for Ethereum that makes it easy to write, test, and deploy smart contracts. In this book, you will learn how to use Truffle to build decentralized applications (DApps) on the Ethereum platform.

Through a combination of lectures, coding exercises, and real-world projects, you will gain the skills and knowledge needed to create your own DApps from scratch. You will learn how to write Solidity contracts, test and debug your contracts with Truffle's powerful tools, and interact with your contracts using web3.js. You will also learn how to deploy your contracts to the Ethereum mainnet and manage them over time.

Whether you are a beginner looking to get started with Blockchain development or an experienced developer looking to expand your skills, this book has something for you. So join us and learn how to harness the power of Truffle to build the next generation of decentralized applications!

WHAT IS TRUFFLE AND WHY USE IT?

Truffle is a popular development framework for Ethereum, a decentralized platform that runs smart contracts: applications that run exactly as programmed without any possibility of downtime, censorship, fraud, or third-party interference.

Truffle is designed to make it easy for developers to build and deploy smart contracts on the Ethereum platform. It provides a suite of tools and libraries that streamline the development process and help developers create high-quality contracts.

Features of Truffle

- **Smart contract compilation:** Truffle can compile your Solidity contracts (the programming language for Ethereum) into bytecode that can be deployed on the Ethereum blockchain. It also generates contract abstractions, which are JavaScript objects that allow you to interact with your contracts from a web app.
- **Test framework:** Truffle includes a powerful test framework that makes it easy to write and run automated tests for your contracts. You can write tests in Solidity or JavaScript, and Truffle will run them on a simulated Ethereum network, giving you fast feedback on the correctness of your contracts.
- **Migration system:** Truffle has a migration system that helps you deploy your contracts to different networks (e.g. the Ethereum mainnet, a testnet, or a local development network). It keeps track of which contracts have been deployed and handles the deployment process for you.
- **Console:** Truffle comes with a console that provides an interactive JavaScript environment for testing and debugging your contracts. You can use the console to execute contract functions, inspect contract state, and more.
- **Built-in security tools:** Truffle includes a number of built-in security tools that help you identify and fix vulnerabilities in your contracts. For example, Truffle has a static analysis tool that can detect potential security issues in your code, and a coverage tool that can help you ensure that your contracts are thoroughly tested.

Benefits of using Truffle

- **Efficiency:** Truffle makes it easy to compile, test, and deploy your contracts, which can save you a lot of time and effort. It also has a lot of built-in features that can help you write better contracts, such as automatic contract abstractions and a test framework.
- **Quality:** Truffle's security tools and testing features can help you catch errors and vulnerabilities in your contracts before they are deployed, which can improve the quality of your contracts and reduce the risk of costly mistakes.

- **Community:** Truffle is a well-established and widely-used development framework, which means that you can benefit from a large and active community of developers who are using and contributing to the project. This can be a valuable resource for getting help, finding examples and solutions, and staying up-to-date with best practices.

Who should use Truffle?

Truffle is a great choice for developers who want to build smart contracts on the Ethereum platform. It is particularly well-suited for those who are new to Ethereum development and want a framework that is easy to learn and use. However, even experienced Ethereum developers can benefit from Truffle's powerful features and security tools.

Conclusion

In summary, Truffle is a development framework that makes it easy to build and deploy smart contracts on the Ethereum platform. It has a wide range of features and benefits that can help developers create high-quality contracts efficiently and effectively. Whether you are a beginner or an experienced Ethereum developer, Truffle is a valuable tool to have in your toolkit.

Exercises

To review these concepts, we will go through a series of exercises designed to test your understanding and apply what you have learned.

What is Truffle used for?
What are some features of Truffle?
What are some benefits of using Truffle?
Who should use Truffle?
True or False: Truffle is a programming language.

Solutions

What is Truffle used for?
Truffle is a development framework for Ethereum, a decentralized platform that runs smart contracts. It is used to make it easy for developers to build and deploy smart contracts on the Ethereum platform.

What are some features of Truffle?
Some features of Truffle include: smart contract compilation, a test framework, a migration system, a console, and built-in security tools.

What are some benefits of using Truffle?
Some benefits of using Truffle include: efficiency, quality, and access to a large and active community of developers.

Who should use Truffle?
Truffle is a good choice for developers who want to build smart contracts on the Ethereum platform, particularly those who are new to Ethereum development. However, even experienced Ethereum developers can benefit from Truffle's powerful features and security tools.

True or False: Truffle is a programming language.

False. Truffle is a development framework, not a programming language. It can be used to compile Solidity contracts (a programming language for Ethereum) into bytecode that can be deployed on the Ethereum blockchain.

SETTING UP A DEVELOPMENT ENVIRONMENT WITH TRUFFLE

Before you can start using Truffle to build smart contracts, you need to set up a development environment. In this tutorial, we will show you how to install and configure Truffle and its dependencies on your machine.

Prerequisites

Before you can set up a Truffle development environment, you need to make sure that you have the following prerequisites installed on your machine:

- **Node.js:** Truffle is built on top of Node.js, so you need to have it installed in order to use Truffle. You can download the latest version of Node.js from the official website (https://nodejs.org/) or through a package manager such as Homebrew (https://brew.sh/) (Mac only).
- **Git:** Git is a version control system that is used to manage the source code for Truffle and its dependencies. You can download Git from the official website (https://git-scm.com/) or through a package manager such as Homebrew (Mac only).
- **Ethereum client:** In order to interact with the Ethereum blockchain, you need to have an Ethereum client installed on your machine. There are several options to choose from, including Go Ethereum (Geth), Parity, and EthereumJS. We recommend using Geth because it is well-maintained and has good documentation. You can download Geth from the official website (https://geth.ethereum.org/) or through a package manager such as Homebrew (Mac only).

Installing Truffle

Now that you have the prerequisites installed, you can install Truffle using npm, the Node.js package manager. Open a terminal window and enter the following command:

```
npm install -g truffle
```

This will install Truffle globally on your machine, which means that you will be able to use it from any directory.

Setting up a Truffle Project

Now that you have Truffle installed, you can create a new Truffle project. To do this, navigate to the directory where you want to create your project and enter the following command:

```
truffle init
```

This will create a new Truffle project in the current directory, with the following directory structure:

```
my-project/
├── contracts/
├── migrations/
├── test/
├── truffle.js
└── truffle-config.js
```

- **contracts/**: This directory contains your Solidity contracts. You can add your contracts to this directory and Truffle will automatically compile them when you run the truffle compile command.
- **migrations/**: This directory contains JavaScript files that handle the deployment of your contracts to the Ethereum network. Truffle uses a migration system to keep track of which contracts have been deployed and to handle the deployment process for you.
- **test/**: This directory contains your contract tests. You can write tests in Solidity or JavaScript and Truffle will run them on a simulated Ethereum network.
- **truffle.js**: This file contains Truffle configuration options, such as the network you want to deploy to and the Ethereum client you are using.
- **truffle-config.js**: This file is similar to truffle.js, but it is used for Truffle versions 5.0 and higher.

Configuring Truffle

Now that you have a Truffle project set up, you need to configure Truffle to use the Ethereum client of your choice. Open the truffle.js or truffle-config.js file (depending on your Truffle version) in a text editor and add the following code:

```
module.exports = {
networks: {
development: {
host: "localhost",
port: 8545,
network_id: "*"
}
}
};
```

This code configures Truffle to use the development network, which is a local Ethereum network that is created using the Ethereum client you installed earlier. The host and port are the network's RPC server address, which Truffle uses to communicate with the Ethereum client. The network_id is the identifier for the network, which Truffle uses to determine which network to deploy to.

Starting the Ethereum Client

Now that you have Truffle configured, you need to start the Ethereum client in order to create the development network. Open a terminal window and enter the following command:

```
geth --dev --rpc --rpcapi "eth,web3,personal"
```

This will start the Geth client in development mode, with the RPC server enabled and the eth, web3, and personal APIs exposed. The development network will be created automatically when you start the client.

Testing the Connection

Now that you have the Ethereum client running and Truffle configured, you can test the connection between Truffle and the Ethereum client. In a separate terminal window, navigate to your Truffle project directory and enter the following command:

```
truffle console
```

This will open the Truffle console, which is an interactive JavaScript environment for testing and debugging your contracts. In the console, enter the following command:

```
web3.version.network
```

If the connection between Truffle and the Ethereum client is working correctly, this command should return the network_id of the development network (e.g. "1337").

Compiling and Deploying Contracts

Now that you have a development environment set up, you can start writing and deploying contracts. To compile your contracts, enter the following command in the Truffle console:

```
truffle compile
```

This will compile your contracts and generate contract abstractions in the build/contracts directory.

To deploy your contracts, you need to create a migration script in the migrations directory. A migration script is a JavaScript file that exports a function that handles the deployment of your contracts. For example, here is a simple migration script that deploys a single contract:

```
const MyContract = artifacts.require("MyContract");
module.exports = function(deployer) {
  deployer.deploy(MyContract);
};
```

To deploy your contracts using this script, enter the following command in the Truffle console:

```
truffle migrate
```

This will run your migration scripts and deploy your contracts to the development network. You can check the status of your deployment by looking at the output of the migrate command or by checking the logs of the Ethereum client.

Conclusion

In this tutorial, we showed you how to set up a development environment with Truffle. You learned how to install and configure Truffle, create a Truffle project, start the Ethereum client, and compile and deploy contracts. With these skills, you are now ready to start building smart contracts with Truffle!

If you have any questions or need further assistance, you can refer to the Truffle documentation (https://truffleframework.com/docs/) or ask for help in the Truffle community (https://truffleframework.com/community). Happy coding!

Exercises

To review these concepts, we will go through a series of exercises designed to test your understanding and apply what you have learned.

What is Truffle?
What are the prerequisites for setting up a Truffle development environment?
How do you install Truffle?
How do you create a Truffle project?
How do you compile and deploy contracts using Truffle?

Solutions

What is Truffle?
Truffle is a development framework for Ethereum, a decentralized platform that runs smart contracts. It is used to make it easy for developers to build and deploy smart contracts on the Ethereum platform.

What are the prerequisites for setting up a Truffle development environment?
The prerequisites for setting up a Truffle development environment are: Node.js, Git, and an Ethereum client (such as Geth).

How do you install Truffle?
To install Truffle, open a terminal window and enter the following command:

```
npm install -g truffle
```

This will install Truffle globally on your machine.

How do you create a Truffle project?
To create a Truffle project, navigate to the directory where you want to create your project and enter the following command:

```
truffle init
```

This will create a new Truffle project in the current directory, with a default directory structure and configuration files.

How do you compile and deploy contracts using Truffle?
To compile contracts using Truffle, open the Truffle console and enter the following command:

truffle compile

This will compile your contracts and generate contract abstractions in the build/contracts directory.

To deploy your contracts, you need to create a migration script in the migrations directory. A migration script is a JavaScript file that exports a function that handles the deployment of your contracts. For example, here is a simple migration script that deploys a single contract:

```javascript
const MyContract = artifacts.require("MyContract");
module.exports = function(deployer) {
  deployer.deploy(MyContract);
};
```

To deploy your contracts using this script, enter the following command in the Truffle console:

truffle migrate

This will run your migration scripts and deploy your contracts to the development network. You can check the status of your deployment by looking at the output of the migrate command or by checking the logs of the Ethereum client.

WRITING SOLIDITY CONTRACTS WITH TRUFFLE

Now that you have set up a development environment with Truffle, you are ready to start writing Solidity contracts. In this tutorial, we will show you how to write, test, and deploy Solidity contracts using Truffle.

What is Solidity?

Solidity is a high-level, contract-oriented programming language for writing smart contracts on the Ethereum platform. It is designed to be statically typed, compiled to bytecode that can be deployed on the Ethereum Virtual Machine (EVM), and to have a syntax similar to that of JavaScript.

Writing a Solidity Contract

To write a Solidity contract with Truffle, you need to create a new Solidity file in the contracts directory of your Truffle project. For example, to create a contract called MyContract, you would create a file called MyContract.sol in the contracts directory.

Here is an example of a simple Solidity contract:

```solidity
pragma solidity ^0.6.0;
contract MyContract {
 string public message;
 constructor() public {
  message = "Hello, world!";
 }
 function setMessage(string memory _message) public {
  message = _message;
 }
}
```

This contract has a single state variable called "message" which is a string that is publicly accessible. It also has a constructor function that is executed when the contract is deployed, and a function called "setMessage" that allows the message to be changed.

Compiling a Solidity Contract

To compile a Solidity contract with Truffle, you need to run the truffle compile command in the

Truffle console. This will compile your contracts and generate contract abstractions in the build/ contracts directory.

For example, to compile the MyContract contract that we defined earlier, you would enter the following command in the Truffle console:

```
truffle compile
```

This will generate a JSON file called MyContract.json in the build/contracts directory, which contains the contract abstraction for MyContract. The contract abstraction is a JavaScript object that contains information about the contract's ABI (Application Binary Interface), bytecode, and deployed address.

Testing a Solidity Contract

To test a Solidity contract with Truffle, you need to create a test file in the test directory of your Truffle project. The test file should export a test function that calls functions on the contract and checks the output to ensure that the contract is behaving as expected.

Here is an example of a test file for the MyContract contract:

```
const MyContract = artifacts.require("MyContract");
contract("MyContract", function() {
  it("should set the message correctly", async function() {
    const instance = await MyContract.deployed();
    await instance.setMessage("Hello, Truffle!");
    const message = await instance.message();
    assert.equal(message, "Hello, Truffle!");
  });
});
```

This test file imports the MyContract contract abstraction, deploys an instance of the contract, and calls the setMessage and message functions to check that the message is correctly set.

To run the test, you can use the truffle test command in the Truffle console. This will compile your contracts, deploy them to a simulated Ethereum network, and run the tests.

For example, to run the test for the MyContract contract, you would enter the following command in the Truffle console:

```
truffle test
```

This will compile your contracts, deploy them to a simulated Ethereum network, and run the tests. If the tests pass, you will see a message indicating that the tests have passed. If the tests fail, you will see an error message indicating which test has failed and why.

Deploying a Solidity Contract

To deploy a Solidity contract with Truffle, you need to create a migration script in the migrations directory. A migration script is a JavaScript file that exports a function that handles the deployment of your contracts.

Here is an example of a migration script that deploys the MyContract contract:

```
const MyContract = artifacts.require("MyContract");
module.exports = function(deployer) {
  deployer.deploy(MyContract);
};
```

To deploy the contract using this script, you can use the truffle migrate command in the Truffle console. This will run the migration scripts and deploy your contracts to the network specified in the Truffle configuration file (e.g. the development network).

For example, to deploy the MyContract contract, you would enter the following command in the Truffle console:

```
truffle migrate
```

This will deploy the contract to the network and output the contract's deployed address. You can then use the contract's address to interact with the contract from your application or from the Truffle console.

Conclusion

In this tutorial, we showed you how to write, test, and deploy Solidity contracts with Truffle. You learned how to create a Solidity contract, compile it with Truffle, write tests for it, and deploy it to the Ethereum network. With these skills, you are now ready to start building your own smart contracts with Truffle!

If you have any questions or need further assistance, you can refer to the Solidity documentation (https://solidity.readthedocs.io/) or ask for help in the Ethereum community (https://ethereum.stackexchange.com/). Happy coding!

Exercises

To review these concepts, we will go through a series of exercises designed to test your understanding and apply what you have learned.

Create a Solidity contract called "HelloWorld" that has a single function called "sayHello" that returns the string "Hello, world!".
Create a Solidity contract called "Bank" that has the following functions:
-"deposit" that allows the caller to deposit ether into the contract
-"withdraw" that allows the caller to withdraw ether from the contract
-"balance" that returns the balance of the contract
-"transfer" that allows the caller to transfer a specified amount of ether to another address
Modify the "Bank" contract from the previous exercise to include the following functions:
-"kill" that allows the owner to kill the contract and send the remaining balance to their account

-"owner" that returns the owner of the contract

Create a Solidity contract called "Token" that has the following functions:

-"mint" that allows the owner to mint a specified amount of tokens and assign them to an account

-"transfer" that allows a token holder to transfer a specified amount of tokens to another account

-"balanceOf" that returns the balance of a specified account

-"totalSupply" that returns the total supply of tokens

Create a Solidity contract called "DonationBox" that has the following functions:

-"donate" that allows a donor to make a donation to the box.

-"withdraw" that allows the owner of the contract to withdraw the total balance of the box.

-"setGoal" that allows the owner of the contract to set a goal for the amount of funds they want to collect.

-"fundsNeeded" that returns the difference between the current balance and the goal.

Solutions

Create a Solidity contract called "HelloWorld" that has a single function called "sayHello" that returns the string "Hello, world!".

```solidity
pragma solidity ^0.6.0;

contract HelloWorld {
  function sayHello() public pure returns (string memory) {
    return "Hello, world!";
  }
}
```

Create a Solidity contract called "Bank" that has the following functions:

-"deposit" that allows the caller to deposit ether into the contract

-"withdraw" that allows the caller to withdraw ether from the contract

-"balance" that returns the balance of the contract

-"transfer" that allows the caller to transfer a specified amount of ether to another address

```solidity
pragma solidity ^0.6.0;

import "https://github.com/OpenZeppelin/openzeppelin-solidity/contracts/utils/SafeMath.sol";

contract Bank {
  using SafeMath for uint;
  mapping(address => uint) public balances;
  uint public totalBalance;
  function deposit() public payable {
    require(msg.value > 0, "Cannot deposit 0 or less ether.");
    balances[msg.sender] = balances[msg.sender].add(msg.value);
    totalBalance = totalBalance.add(msg.value);
  }
  function withdraw(uint amount) public {
```

```
    require(amount <= balances[msg.sender], "Insufficient balance.");
    require(amount > 0, "Cannot withdraw 0 or less ether.");
    balances[msg.sender] = balances[msg.sender].sub(amount);
    totalBalance = totalBalance.sub(amount);
    msg.sender.transfer(amount);
  }
  function balance(address account) public view returns (uint) {
    return balances[account];
  }
  function transfer(address recipient, uint amount) public {
    require(amount <= balances[msg.sender], "Insufficient balance.");
    require(amount > 0, "Cannot transfer 0 or less ether.");
    balances[msg.sender] = balances[msg.sender].sub(amount);
    balances[recipient] = balances[recipient].add(amount);
  }
}
```

Modify the "Bank" contract from the previous exercise to include the following functions:
-"kill" that allows the owner to kill the contract and send the remaining balance to their account
-"owner" that returns the owner of the contract

```
pragma solidity ^0.6.0;
import "https://github.com/OpenZeppelin/openzeppelin-solidity/contracts/utils/SafeMath.sol";
contract Bank {
  using SafeMath for uint;
  mapping(address => uint) public balances;
  uint public totalBalance;
  address public owner;
  constructor() public {
    owner = msg.sender;
  }
  function deposit() public payable {
    require(msg.value > 0, "Cannot deposit 0 or less ether.");
    balances[msg.sender] = balances[msg.sender].add(msg.value);
    totalBalance = totalBalance.add(msg.value);
  }
  function withdraw(uint amount) public {
    require(amount <= balances[msg.sender], "Insufficient balance.");
```

```solidity
    require(amount > 0, "Cannot withdraw 0 or less ether.");

    balances[msg.sender] = balances[msg.sender].sub(amount);

    totalBalance = totalBalance.sub(amount);

    msg.sender.transfer(amount);

}

function balance(address account) public view returns (uint) {

    return balances[account];

}

function transfer(address recipient, uint amount) public {

    require(amount <= balances[msg.sender], "Insufficient balance.");

    require(amount > 0, "Cannot transfer 0 or less ether.");

    balances[msg.sender] = balances[msg.sender].sub(amount);

    balances[recipient] = balances[recipient].add(amount);

}

function kill() public {

    require(msg.sender == owner, "Only the owner can kill the contract.");

    selfdestruct(owner);

}

}
```

Create a Solidity contract called "Token" that has the following functions:
- "mint" that allows the owner to mint a specified amount of tokens and assign them to an account
- "transfer" that allows a token holder to transfer a specified amount of tokens to another account
- "balanceOf" that returns the balance of a specified account
- "totalSupply" that returns the total supply of tokens

```solidity
pragma solidity ^0.6.0;

import "https://github.com/OpenZeppelin/openzeppelin-solidity/contracts/utils/SafeMath.sol";

contract Auction {

    using SafeMath for uint;

    struct Item {

        address owner;

        uint price;

    }

    Item public item;

    address public highestBidder;

    uint public highestBid;

    constructor(address _owner, uint _price) public {
```

```solidity
    item.owner = _owner;
    item.price = _price;
  }
  function bid() public payable {
    require(msg.value > highestBid, "Bid must be higher than current highest bid.");
    require(msg.value > item.price, "Bid must be higher than the minimum price.");
    if (highestBidder != address(0)) {
      highestBidder.transfer(highestBid);
    }
    highestBidder = msg.sender;
    highestBid = msg.value;
  }
  function withdraw() public {
    require(msg.sender == highestBidder, "Only the current highest bidder can withdraw their bid.");
    msg.sender.transfer(highestBid);
    highestBidder = address(0);
    highestBid = 0;
  }
  function auctionEnd() public {
    require(msg.sender == item.owner, "Only the owner can end the auction.");
    require(highestBidder != address(0), "There must be a highest bidder to end the auction.");
    item.owner.transfer(highestBid);
    delete item;
  }
}
```

Create a Solidity contract called "DonationBox" that has the following functions:
-"donate" that allows a donor to make a donation to the box.
-"withdraw" that allows the owner of the contract to withdraw the total balance of the box.
-"setGoal" that allows the owner of the contract to set a goal for the amount of funds they want to collect.
-"fundsNeeded" that returns the difference between the current balance and the goal.

```solidity
pragma solidity ^0.6.0;
import "https://github.com/OpenZeppelin/openzeppelin-solidity/contracts/utils/SafeMath.sol";
contract DonationBox {
  using SafeMath for uint;
  address public owner;
  uint public balance;
```

```solidity
uint public goal;
constructor() public {
    owner = msg.sender;
}
function donate() public payable {
    balance = balance.add(msg.value);
}
function withdraw() public {
    require(msg.sender == owner, "Only the owner can withdraw funds.");
    msg.sender.transfer(balance);
    balance = 0;
}
function setGoal(uint _goal) public {
    require(msg.sender == owner, "Only the owner can set the goal.");
    goal = _goal;
}
function fundsNeeded() public view returns (uint) {
    return goal.sub(balance);
}
}
```

TESTING CONTRACTS WITH TRUFFLE'S TEST FRAMEWORK

In the previous tutorial, we showed you how to write, test, and deploy Solidity contracts with Truffle. In this tutorial, we will dive deeper into Truffle's testing features and show you how to use the Truffle test framework to write more advanced tests for your contracts.

What is Truffle's Test Framework?

Truffle's test framework is a testing library that is bundled with Truffle and used to write and run tests for Ethereum contracts. It is built on top of the Mocha testing framework and includes a suite of utility functions and assertion libraries that are specific to Ethereum.

Writing Tests with Truffle's Test Framework

To write a test with Truffle's test framework, you need to create a test file in the test directory of your Truffle project. The test file should export a test function that calls functions on the contract and checks the output to ensure that the contract is behaving as expected.

Here is an example of a test file that tests the MyContract contract from the previous tutorial:

```
const MyContract = artifacts.require("MyContract");
contract("MyContract", function() {
  it("should set the message correctly", async function() {
    const instance = await MyContract.deployed();
    await instance.setMessage("Hello, Truffle!");
    const message = await instance.message();
    assert.equal(message, "Hello, Truffle!");
  });
});
```

This test file imports the MyContract contract abstraction, deploys an instance of the contract, and calls the setMessage and message functions to check that the message is correctly set.

To run the test, you can use the truffle test command in the Truffle console. This will compile your contracts, deploy them to a simulated Ethereum network, and run the tests.

For example, to run the test for the MyContract contract, you would enter the following command in the Truffle console:

Using Truffle's Utility Functions

Truffle's test framework includes a suite of utility functions that you can use to write more advanced tests for your contracts. These functions allow you to manipulate the state of the Ethereum network, create and deploy contracts, and interact with contracts in various ways.

Here are some examples of Truffle's utility functions:

- web3.eth.getBalance(address): Returns the balance of the specified Ethereum account in wei.
- web3.eth.sendTransaction({from, to, value}): Sends a transaction from the from account to the to account with the specified value in wei.
- web3.eth.getTransactionReceipt(transactionHash): Returns the receipt of the transaction with the specified transaction hash.
- web3.eth.getBlock(blockHashOrBlockNumber): Returns the block with the specified block hash or block number.

You can use these utility functions in your tests to simulate various scenarios and test the behavior of your contracts. For example, you can use web3.eth.sendTransaction to send transactions to your contract and test its functionality, or use web3.eth.getBlock to check the block timestamp and test time-dependent functionality.

Using Truffle's Assertion Libraries

Truffle's test framework also includes a set of assertion libraries that you can use to write assertions in your tests. These libraries provide a variety of assertion functions that you can use to check the values of variables and the state of the Ethereum network.

Here are some examples of Truffle's assertion libraries:

- assert.equal(actual, expected): Asserts that the actual value is equal to the expected value.
- assert.notEqual(actual, expected): Asserts that the actual value is not equal to the expectedvalue.
- assert.isTrue(value): Asserts that the value is true.
- assert.isFalse(value): Asserts that the value is false.

You can use these assertion functions in your tests to check the output of your contracts and ensure that they are behaving as expected. For example, you can use assert.equal to check that the value returned by a contract function is correct, or use assert.isTrue to check that a boolean value is true.

Conclusion

In this tutorial, we showed you how to use Truffle's test framework to write advanced tests for your contracts. You learned how to write tests with Truffle's test framework, use Truffle's utility functions to manipulate the Ethereum network, and use Truffle's assertion libraries to write assertions in your tests. With these skills, you are now ready to write robust tests for your contracts and ensure that they are functioning correctly.

If you have any questions or need further assistance, you can refer to the Truffle documentation (https://truffleframework.com/docs/) or ask for help in the Truffle community (https://truffleframework.com/community). Happy coding!

Exercises

To review these concepts, we will go through a series of exercises designed to test your understanding and apply what you have learned.

How do you compile and deploy contracts using Truffle?
How do you write a test with Truffle's test framework?
Write a test using Truffle's test framework that checks if the value of a contract's balance **variable is equal to 100.**
Write a test using Truffle's test framework that sends a transaction from account A to account B and checks if the balance of account B is increased by the value of the transaction.
Write a test using Truffle's test framework that calls a contract function that requires a certain amount of gas and checks if the contract's gas usage is within the expected range.

Solutions

How do you compile and deploy contracts using Truffle?
To compile contracts using Truffle, open the Truffle console and enter the following command:

```
truffle compile
```

This will compile your contracts and generate contract abstractions in the build/contracts directory.

To deploy your contracts, you need to create a migration script in the migrations directory. A migration script is a JavaScript file that exports a function that handles the deployment of your contracts. For example, here is a simple migration script that deploys a single contract:

```
const MyContract = artifacts.require("MyContract");
module.exports = function(deployer) {
  deployer.deploy(MyContract);
};
```

To deploy your contracts using this script, enter the following command in the Truffle console:

```
truffle migrate
```

This will run your migration scripts and deploy your contracts to the development network. You can check the status of your deployment by looking at the output of the migrate command or by checking the logs of the Ethereum client.

How do you write a test with Truffle's test framework?
To write a test with Truffle's test framework, you need to create a test file in the test directory of your Truffle project. The test file should export a test function that calls functions on the contract and checks the output to ensure that the contract is behaving as expected.

Here is an example of a test file that tests the MyContract contract:

```
const MyContract = artifacts.require("MyContract");
contract("MyContract", function() {
it("should set the message correctly", async function() {
  const instance = await MyContract.deployed();
  await instance.setMessage("Hello, Truffle!");
  const message = await instance.message();
  assert.equal(message, "Hello, Truffle!");
});
});
```

This test file imports the MyContract contract abstraction, deploys an instance of the contract, and calls the setMessage and message functions to check that the message is correctly set.

To run the test, you can use the truffle test command in the Truffle console. This will compile your contracts, deploy them to a simulated Ethereum network, and run the tests.

Write a test using Truffle's test framework that checks if the value of a contract's balance variable is equal to 100.

To write a test that checks if the value of a contract's balance variable is equal to 100, you can use Truffle's assert.equal function. This function allows you to compare the actual value of the balancevariable to the expected value of 100.

Here is an example of a test that checks if the value of a contract's balance variable is equal to 100:

```
const MyContract = artifacts.require("MyContract");
contract("MyContract", function() {
it("should have a balance of 100", async function() {
  const instance = await MyContract.deployed();
  const balance = await instance.balance();
  assert.equal(balance, 100);
});
});
```

This test file imports the MyContract contract abstraction, deploys an instance of the contract, and calls the balance function to get the value of the balance variable. It then uses the assert.equalfunction to compare the value of the balance variable to the expected value of 100.

To run this test, you can use the truffle test command in the Truffle console. This will compile your contracts, deploy them to a simulated Ethereum network, and run the tests. If the test passes, you will see a message indicating that the test has passed. If the test fails, you will see an error message indicating that the test has failed and the expected and actual values of the balance variable.

Write a test using Truffle's test framework that sends a transaction from account A to account B and checks if the balance of account B is increased by the value of the transaction.

To write a test that sends a transaction from account A to account B and checks if the balance of account B is increased by the value of the transaction, you can use Truffle's web3.eth.sendTransaction function to send the transaction and Truffle's assert.equal function to compare the actual and expected balances of account B.

Here is an example of a test that sends a transaction from account A to account B and checks if the balance of account B is increased by the value of the transaction:

```
const MyContract = artifacts.require("MyContract");
contract("MyContract", function() {
  it("should increase the balance of account B by the value of the transaction", async function() {
    const instance = await MyContract.deployed();
    const initialBalance = await web3.eth.getBalance(accountB);
    await web3.eth.sendTransaction({from: accountA, to: accountB, value: 100});
    const finalBalance = await web3.eth.getBalance(accountB);
    assert.equal(finalBalance, initialBalance + 100);
  });
});
```

This test file imports the MyContract contract abstraction, deploys an instance of the contract, and uses the web3.eth.getBalance function to get the initial and final balances of account B. It then uses the web3.eth.sendTransaction function to send a transaction from account A to account B with a value of 100 wei. Finally, it uses the assert.equal function to compare the final balance of account B to the expected balance (initial balance + 100 wei).

To run this test, you can use the truffle test command in the Truffle console. This will compile your contracts, deploy them to a simulated Ethereum network, and run the tests. If the test passes, you will see a message indicating that the test has passed. If the test fails, you will see an error message indicating that the test has failed and the expected and actual values of the balance of account B.

Write a test using Truffle's test framework that calls a contract function that requires a certain amount of gas and checks if the contract's gas usage is within the expected range.

To write a test that calls a contract function that requires a certain amount of gas and checks if the contract's gas usage is within the expected range, you can use Truffle's web3.eth.getTransactionReceipt function to get the receipt of the transaction and Truffle's assert.isBelow function to check if the gas used is within the expected range.

Here is an example of a test that calls a contract function that requires a certain amount of gas and checks if the contract's gas usage is within the expected range:

```
const MyContract = artifacts.require("MyContract");
contract("MyContract", function() {
```

```
it("should use a reasonable amount of gas", async function() {
  const instance = await MyContract.deployed();
  const receipt = await web3.eth.getTransactionReceipt(await instance.expensiveFunction());
  assert.isBelow(receipt.gasUsed, 1000000);
});
});
```

This test file imports the MyContract contract abstraction, deploys an instance of the contract, and calls the expensiveFunction function. It then uses the web3.eth.getTransactionReceipt function to get the receipt of the transaction and uses the assert.isBelow function to check if the gas used is less than 1 million.

To run this test, you can use the truffle test command in the Truffle console. This will compile your contracts, deploy them to a simulated Ethereum network, and run the tests. If the test passes, you will see a message indicating that the test has passed. If the test fails, you will see an error message indicating that the test has failed and the expected and actual values of the gas used.

DEBUGGING CONTRACTS WITH TRUFFLE

Debugging contracts can be a challenging task, especially when you are working with complex contracts that interact with other contracts or the Ethereum network. Truffle provides a variety of tools and features that you can use to debug your contracts and find and fix issues more efficiently.

In this tutorial, we will show you how to use Truffle's debugging tools and techniques to troubleshoot your contracts and resolve issues. We will cover the following topics:

- Using Truffle's debugging commands
- Debugging transactions with Remix and the Truffle Debugger
- Debugging contract calls with the Truffle Console
- Debugging events with Truffle's event tracking feature

Using Truffle's Debugging Commands

Truffle provides several commands that you can use to debug your contracts and the Ethereum network. These commands allow you to inspect the state of your contracts, the blocks and transactions on the network, and other relevant information.

Here are some examples of Truffle's debugging commands:

- truffle debug <transactionHash>: Opens the Truffle Debugger and allows you to debug the transaction with the specified transaction hash.
- truffle inspect <contractName>: Prints the ABI and deployed address of the contract with the specified contract name.
- truffle networks: Shows the available networks and their configurations.
- truffle console: Opens the Truffle Console, which allows you to interact with the Ethereum network and your contracts.

You can use these commands to gather information about your contracts and the Ethereum network and identify potential issues. For example, you can use the truffle debug command to debug a transaction that failed or the truffle console command to call contract functions and check their output.

Debugging Transactions with Remix and the Truffle Debugger

Remix is an online code editor and compiler for Solidity contracts. It includes a built-in debugger that you can use to step through the execution of your contracts and inspect the state of the Ethereum network and your contracts.

To debug a transaction with Remix and the Truffle Debugger, follow these steps:

1. Go to https://remix.ethereum.org and open the Solidity contract that you want to debug.
2. Click the "Debug" button in the top menu.
3. In the "Debugger" panel, select the contract that you want to debug and the function that you want to call.
4. Enter the input values for the function and click the "Create Transaction" button.
5. In the "Debugging" panel, click the "Start Debugging" button.
6. Use the controls in the "Debugging" panel to step through the execution of the contract and inspect the state of the Ethereum network and your contracts.

You can use Remix and the Truffle Debugger to debug transactions and identify issues with your contracts. For example, you can use the Truffle Debugger to inspect the variables and storage of your contracts and check if they have the expected values.

Debugging Contract Calls with the Truffle Console

The Truffle Console is a command-line interface (CLI) that allows you to interact with the Ethereum network and your contracts. You can use the Truffle Console to call contract functions, send transactions, and inspect the state of your contracts.

To open the Truffle Console, enter the following command in your terminal:

```
truffle console
```

This will open the Truffle Console and connect it to the Ethereum network. You can then use the Truffle Console to call contract functions and inspect the state of your contracts.

Here is an example of how you can use the Truffle Console to call a contract function and inspect the output:

```
// Import the contract abstraction
const MyContract = artifacts.require("MyContract");
// Deploy an instance of the contract
const instance = await MyContract.deployed();
// Call the getValue function of the contract
const value = await instance.getValue();
// Print the output of the function
console.log(value);
```

You can use the Truffle Console to debug contract calls and identify issues with your contracts. For example, you can use the Truffle Console to call contract functions with different input values and check if they produce the expected output.

Debugging events with Truffle's Event Tracking Feature

Events are a way for contracts to communicate with the Ethereum network and external clients.

Contracts can emit events when certain actions are performed, and external clients can listen for and react to these events.

Truffle provides a feature called "event tracking" that allows you to track and debug events emitted by your contracts. To use event tracking, you need to specify the events that you want to track in your Truffle configuration file (truffle-config.js).

Here is an example of how you can use event tracking to track the "ValueChanged" event of the MyContract contract:

```
module.exports = {
// ...
events: {
  MyContract: ["ValueChanged"]
}
// ...
};
```

Once you have configured event tracking, you can use the Truffle Console to listen for and debug events emitted by your contracts.

To listen for events, you can use the .on method of the contract instance:

```
instance.on("ValueChanged", (value, event) => {
  console.log(`Value changed: ${value}`);
});
```

This will print the value of the "ValueChanged" event every time it is emitted by the contract. You can use event tracking to debug events and identify issues with your contracts.

Conclusion

In conclusion, Truffle provides a variety of tools and features that you can use to debug your contracts and resolve issues. You can use Truffle's debugging commands to gather information about your contracts and the Ethereum network, Remix and the Truffle Debugger to debug transactions, the Truffle Console to debug contract calls, and Truffle's event tracking feature to debug events. By using these tools and techniques, you can troubleshoot your contracts and ensure that they are working as expected.

If you have any questions or need further assistance, you can refer to the Truffle documentation (https://truffleframework.com/docs/) or ask for help in the Truffle community (https://truffleframework.com/community). Happy coding!

Exercises

To review these concepts, we will go through a series of exercises designed to test your understanding and apply what you have learned.

Use Truffle's truffle debug **command to debug a transaction that failed. Inspect the variables and storage of the contract and identify the issue.**

Use Remix and the Truffle Debugger to debug a transaction and identify the cause of the error.

Use the Truffle Console to call a contract function with different input values and check if it produces the expected output.

Use Truffle's event tracking feature to track and debug an event emitted by a contract.

Write a test using Truffle's test framework that checks if a contract function emits the expected event.

Solutions

Use Truffle's truffle debug **command to debug a transaction that failed. Inspect the variables and storage of the contract and identify the issue.**

To use Truffle's truffle debug command to debug a transaction that failed, follow these steps:

- Run the truffle debug <transactionHash> command in the Truffle console, replacing <transactionHash> with the transaction hash of the failed transaction.
- Use the controls in the debugger to step through the execution of the contract and inspect the variables and storage.
- Identify the issue by examining the values of the variables and storage and comparing them to the expected values.

Use Remix and the Truffle Debugger to debug a transaction and identify the cause of the error.

To use Remix and the Truffle Debugger to debug a transaction and identify the cause of the error, follow these steps:

- Go to https://remix.ethereum.org and open the Solidity contract that you want to debug.
- Click the "Debug" button in the top menu.
- In the "Debugger" panel, select the contract that you want to debug and the function that you want to call.
- Enter the input values for the function and click the "Create Transaction" button.
- In the "Debugging" panel, click the "Start Debugging" button.
- Use the controls in the "Debugging" panel to step through the execution of the contract and inspect the variables and storage.
- Identify the cause of the error by examining the values of the variables and storage and comparing them to the expected values.

Use the Truffle Console to call a contract function with different input values and check if it produces the expected output.

To use the Truffle Console to call a contract function with different input values and check if it produces the expected output, follow these steps:

- Open the Truffle Console by running the truffle console command in your terminal.
- Import the contract abstraction and deploy an instance of the contract.
- Call the contract function with different input values and use the console.log function to print the output.

- Compare the output to the expected output and identify any issues.

Here is an example of how you can do this:

```
// Import the contract abstraction
const MyContract = artifacts.require("MyContract");
// Deploy an instance of the contract
const instance = await MyContract.deployed();
// Call the contract function with different input values
const output1 = await instance.myFunction(1);
const output2 = await instance.myFunction(2);
// Print the output of the function
console.log(output1);
console.log(output2);
```

Use Truffle's event tracking feature to track and debug an event emitted by a contract.

To use Truffle's event tracking feature to track and debug an event emitted by a contract, follow these steps:

- Configure event tracking in your Truffle configuration file (truffle-config.js) by specifying the events that you want to track.
- Open the Truffle Console by running the truffle console command in your terminal.
- Import the contract abstraction and deploy an instance of the contract.
- Use the .on method of the contract instance to listen for the event.
- Use the console.log function to print the output of the event.
- Identify any issues by comparing the output of the event to the expected output.

Here is an example of how you can do this:

```
// Import the contract abstraction
const MyContract = artifacts.require("MyContract");
// Deploy an instance of the contract
const instance = await MyContract.deployed();
// Listen for the event
instance.on("MyEvent", (value, event) => {
  console.log(`MyEvent emitted: ${value}`);
});
```

Write a test using Truffle's test framework that checks if a contract function emits the expected event.

To write a test using Truffle's test framework that checks if a contract function emits the expected event, follow these steps:

- Write a test file that imports the contract abstraction and deploys an instance of the

contract.
- Use the .on method of the contract instance to listen for the event.
- Call the contract function that is supposed to emit the event.
- Use the assert function to check if the event was emitted.

Here is an example of how you can do this:

```
const MyContract = artifacts.require("MyContract");
contract("MyContract", function() {
  it("should emit MyEvent", async function() {
    // Deploy an instance of the contract
    const instance = await MyContract.deployed();
    // Listen for the event
    let eventEmitted = false;
    instance.on("MyEvent", (value, event) => {
      eventEmitted = true;
    });
    // Call the contract function that is supposed to emit the event
    await instance.myFunction();
    // Check if the event was emitted
    assert.isTrue(eventEmitted, "MyEvent was not emitted");
  });
});
```

This test will deploy an instance of the MyContract contract and listen for the MyEvent event. It will then call the myFunction function of the contract and check if the MyEvent event was emitted. If the event was not emitted, the test will fail.

CONNECTING TO AN ETHEREUM NETWORK WITH WEB3.JS AND TRUFFLE

One of the key features of Truffle is its integration with web3.js, a JavaScript library that allows you to interact with the Ethereum network. By using web3.js and Truffle together, you can easily connect to an Ethereum network and start working with your contracts.

In this chapter, we will look at how you can use web3.js and Truffle to connect to an Ethereum network and work with your contracts. We will also look at some best practices for working with web3.js and Truffle in a development environment.

Installing Web3.js and Truffle

Before you can start using web3.js and Truffle, you need to install them on your development machine. To install web3.js, you can use the following command:

```
npm install web3
```

To install Truffle, you can use the following command:

```
npm install -g truffle
```

Once you have installed web3.js and Truffle, you can start using them to connect to an Ethereum network and work with your contracts.

Connecting to an Ethereum Network with Web3.js

To connect to an Ethereum network with web3.js, you need to create a new Web3 instance and specify the network that you want to connect to. There are several ways you can do this, depending on the network you want to connect to and the environment you are working in.

Here are some examples of how you can connect to different networks with web3.js:

Connecting to a Local Development Network

To connect to a local development network such as Ganache, you can use the following code:

```javascript
const Web3 = require("web3");
// Connect to the local development network
const web3 = new Web3("http://localhost:7545");
```

This will create a new Web3 instance and connect it to the local development network running on port 7545.

Connecting to the Ethereum Mainnet

To connect to the Ethereum mainnet, you can use the following code:

```
const Web3 = require("web3");
// Connect to the Ethereum mainnet
const web3 = new Web3("https://mainnet.infura.io");
```

This will create a new Web3 instance and connect it to the Ethereum mainnet using Infura, a service that provides access to the Ethereum network.

Connecting to a Custom Network

To connect to a custom network, you can use the following code:

```
const Web3 = require("web3");
// Connect to a custom network
const web3 = new Web3("http://<your-custom-network>:7545");
```

This will create a new Web3 instance and connect it to the custom network running on port 7545.

Working with Contracts in Truffle

Once you have connected to an Ethereum network with web3.js, you can use Truffle to work with your contracts. Truffle provides a variety of commands and features that you can use to deploy, test, and debug your contracts.

Here are some examples of how you can use Truffle to work with your contracts:

Deploying Contracts

To deploy a contract with Truffle, you can use the following command:

```
truffle deploy
```

This will deploy all of your contracts to the Ethereum network that you are connected to. You can also specify a specific contract to deploy by using the --contract flag, like this:

```
truffle deploy --contract MyContract
```

Testing Contracts

To test a contract with Truffle, you can use the following command:

```
truffle test
```

This will run all of your contract tests and display the results. You can also specify a specific test file to run by using the --file flag, like this:

```
truffle test --file MyTest.js
```

Debugging Contracts

To debug a contract with Truffle, you can use the following command:

```
truffle debug <transactionHash>
```

This will open the Truffle Debugger and allow you to step through the execution of a transaction. You can inspect the variables and storage of the contract and identify the cause of any issues.

Best Practices for Working with Web3.js and Truffle

Here are some best practices for working with web3.js and Truffle:

- Use a local development network such as Ganache while developing your contracts. This will allow you to test and debug your contracts without incurring real Ethereum fees.
- Use the Truffle Console to interact with your contracts in a development environment. This will allow you to test and debug your contracts without writing any code.
- Use Truffle's test framework to write automated tests for your contracts. This will help you ensure that your contracts are working as expected and catch any issues early on.
- Use Truffle's debugging tools, such as the Truffle Debugger and the Truffle Console, to troubleshoot issues with your contracts.
- Use web3.js and Truffle in combination to deploy and interact with your contracts on the Ethereum network.

By following these best practices, you can streamline your contract development process and ensure that your contracts are working as expected.

Conclusion

In this chapter, we looked at how you can use web3.js and Truffle to connect to an Ethereum network and work with your contracts. We covered different ways of connecting to different networks with web3.js, and we looked at how you can use Truffle to deploy, test, and debug your contracts. We also discussed some best practices for working with web3.js and Truffle in a development environment.

By using web3.js and Truffle together, you can easily connect to an Ethereum network and start working with your contracts. This can save you a lot of time and effort, and help you streamline your contract development process.

If you have any questions or need further assistance, you can refer to the Truffle documentation (https://truffleframework.com/docs/) or ask for help in the Truffle community (https://truffleframework.com/community). Happy coding!

Exercises

To review these concepts, we will go through a series of exercises designed to test your understanding and apply what you have learned.

Write a script that connects to the Ethereum mainnet using web3.js and prints the current block number.

Write a Truffle test that deploys an instance of a contract and checks if it was deployed

successfully.
Write a script that uses the Truffle Console to interact with a deployed contract.
Write a Truffle test that calls a contract function and checks if it emits the expected event.
Write a script that uses the Truffle Debugger to debug a contract transaction.

Solutions

Write a script that connects to the Ethereum mainnet using web3.js and prints the current block number.

```
const Web3 = require("web3");
// Connect to the Ethereum mainnet
const web3 = new Web3("https://mainnet.infura.io");
// Get the current block number
web3.eth.getBlockNumber((error, result) => {
 console.log(`Current block number: ${result}`);
});
```

Write a Truffle test that deploys an instance of a contract and checks if it was deployed successfully.

```
const MyContract = artifacts.require("MyContract");
contract("MyContract", function() {
 it("should be deployed", async function() {
  // Deploy an instance of the contract
  const instance = await MyContract.new();
  // Check if the contract was deployed
  assert.isNotNull(instance.address, "Contract was not deployed");
 });
});
```

Write a script that uses the Truffle Console to interact with a deployed contract.

```
// Load the contract abstraction
const MyContract = artifacts.require("MyContract");
// Connect to the deployed instance of the contract
MyContract.at("0x123...").then(instance => {
 // Call a contract function
 instance.myFunction().then(result => {
  console.log(result);
 });
});
```

Write a Truffle test that calls a contract function and checks if it emits the expected event.

```javascript
const MyContract = artifacts.require("MyContract");
contract("MyContract", function() {
  it("should emit MyEvent", async function() {
    // Deploy an instance of the contract
    const instance = await MyContract.deployed();
    // Listen for the event
    let eventEmitted = false;
    instance.on("MyEvent", (value, event) => {
      eventEmitted = true;
    });
    // Call the contract function that is supposed to emit the event
    await instance.myFunction();
    // Check if the event was emitted
    assert.isTrue(eventEmitted, "MyEvent was not emitted");
  });
});
```

Write a script that uses the Truffle Debugger to debug a contract transaction.

```javascript
// Load the contract abstraction
const MyContract = artifacts.require("MyContract");
// Connect to the deployed instance of the contract
MyContract.at("0x123...").then(instance => {
  // Start the debugger
  debugger;
  // Call a contract function
  instance.myFunction().then(result => {
    console.log(result);
  });
});
```

INTERACTING WITH SMART CONTRACTS FROM A WEB APP USING TRUFFLE AND WEB3.JS

In the previous chapters of this course, we looked at how you can use Truffle and web3.js to connect to an Ethereum network and work with your contracts. Now, we will look at how you can use these tools to build a web app that interacts with your smart contracts.

By using Truffle and web3.js to build a web app, you can create a user-friendly interface for your smart contracts that can be accessed from any device with a web browser. This can make it easier for users to interact with your contracts and benefit from their functionality.

In this chapter, we will look at how you can use Truffle and web3.js to build a web app that interacts with your smart contracts. We will also look at some best practices for building web apps with Truffle and web3.js.

Setting Up a Project with Truffle and Web3.js

To build a web app with Truffle and web3.js, you need to set up a project that includes both tools. Here's how you can do this:

1. Create a new project folder and navigate to it in your terminal.
2. Run the truffle init command to initialize a new Truffle project. This will create a truffle-config.js file and a contracts folder in your project.
3. Run the npm init command to initialize a new Node.js project. This will create a package.json file in your project.
4. Install web3.js by running the npm install web3 command.

Once you have set up your project with Truffle and web3.js, you can start building your web app.

Building a Web App with Truffle and Web3.js

To build a web app with Truffle and web3.js, you need to do the following:

1. Write your smart contracts using Solidity and compile them with Truffle.
2. Deploy your contracts to an Ethereum network using Truffle.
3. Connect to the Ethereum network and your deployed contracts using web3.js.
4. Write the front-end code for your web app using HTML, CSS, and JavaScript. This code should use web3.js to interact with your deployed contracts and display the results to the user.

Here is an example of how you can use web3.js to interact with a deployed contract in your web app:

```
const Web3 = require("web3");
// Connect to the Ethereum network
const web3 = new Web3("https://mainnet.infura.io");
// Load the contract abstraction
const MyContract = require("../build/contracts/MyContract.json");
// Get the address of the deployed contract
const contractAddress = "0x123...";
// Connect to the deployed contract
const instance = new web3.eth.Contract(
  MyContract.abi,
  contractAddress
);
// Call a contract function
instance.methods.myFunction().call((error, result) => {
  console.log(result);
});
```

In this example, we are using web3.js to connect to the Ethereum mainnet and load the contract abstraction for our MyContract contract. We then get the address of the deployed contract and use it to connect to the deployed instance of the contract. Finally, we call the myFunction function of the contract and print the result to the console.

Best Practices for building Web Apps with Truffle and Web3.js

Here are some best practices for building web apps with Truffle and web3.js:

- Use a local development network such as Ganache while developing your web app. This will allow you to test and debug your app without incurring real Ethereum fees.
- Use Truffle to compile and deploy your contracts. This will ensure that your contracts are deployed consistently and correctly.
- Use web3.js to connect to the Ethereum network and interact with your contracts. This will allow you to easily access the functionality of your contracts from your web app.
- Use the MetaMask browser extension to allow users to interact with your web app using their Ethereum accounts. This will make it easier for users to use your app and will enhance their security.

By following these best practices, you can build a web app that is easy to use and interact with your smart contracts in a reliable and secure way.

Conclusion

In this chapter, we looked at how you can use Truffle and web3.js to build a web app that interacts with your smart contracts. We covered the steps involved in setting up a project with Truffle and web3.js and building a web app with these tools. We also discussed some best practices for building web apps with Truffle and web3.js.

By using Truffle and web3.js to build a web app, you can create a user-friendly interface for your smart contracts that can be accessed from any device with a web browser. This can make it easier for users to interact with your contracts and benefit from their functionality.

If you have any questions or need further assistance, you can refer to the Truffle documentation (https://truffleframework.com/docs/) or ask for help in the Truffle community (https://truffleframework.com/community). Happy coding!

Exercises

To review these concepts, we will go through a series of exercises designed to test your understanding and apply what you have learned.

Write a Truffle migration script that deploys a contract and stores its address in a JSON file.
Write a web3.js script that reads the contract address from a JSON file and connects to the deployed contract.
Write a web app that displays a list of contract functions and allows the user to call them.
Write a Truffle test that checks if a contract function calls another contract function correctly.
Write a web app that allows the user to interact with a contract using a form.

Solutions

Write a Truffle migration script that deploys a contract and stores its address in a JSON file.

```javascript
const MyContract = artifacts.require("MyContract");
module.exports = function(deployer) {
 deployer.deploy(MyContract).then(() => {
  // Store the contract's address in a JSON file
  const contractAddress = MyContract.address;
  const contractAddressJson = { contractAddress };
  fs.writeFileSync(
   "contract-address.json",
   JSON.stringify(contractAddressJson, null, 2)
  );
 });
};
```

Write a web3.js script that reads the contract address from a JSON file and connects to the deployed contract.

```javascript
const Web3 = require("web3");
// Connect to the Ethereum network
```

```
const web3 = new Web3("https://mainnet.infura.io");
// Load the contract address from a JSON file
const contractAddressJson = JSON.parse(fs.readFileSync("contract-address.json"));
const contractAddress = contractAddressJson.contractAddress;
// Load the contract abstraction
const MyContract = require("../build/contracts/MyContract.json");
// Connect to the deployed contract
const instance = new web3.eth.Contract(
  MyContract.abi,
  contractAddress
);
// Call a contract function
instance.methods.myFunction().call((error, result) => {
  console.log(result);
});
```

Write a web app that displays a list of contract functions and allows the user to call them.

```
<!-- Display a list of contract functions -->
<ul>
  <li>
    <button onclick="callFunction('myFunction')">My Function</button>
  </li>
  <li>
    <button onclick="callFunction('myOtherFunction')">My Other Function</button>
  </li>
</ul>
<!-- Display the result of the called function -->
<div id="result"></div>
<script>
  // Connect to the Ethereum network and the deployed contract
  const web3 = new Web3("https://mainnet.infura.io");
  const contractAddress = "0x123...";
  const contract = new web3.eth.Contract(abi, contractAddress);
  // Call a contract function
  function callFunction(functionName) {
    contract.methods[functionName]().call((error, result) => {
      document.getElementById("result").innerHTML = result;
```

```
  });

}

</script>
```

Write a Truffle test that checks if a contract function calls another contract function correctly.

```javascript
const MyContract = artifacts.require("MyContract");

const OtherContract = artifacts.require("OtherContract");

contract("MyContract", function() {

it("should call OtherContract's function correctly", async function() {

  // Deploy instances of both contracts

  const myContract = await MyContract.deployed();

  const otherContract = await OtherContract.deployed();

  // Set up a mock for OtherContract's function

  const mock = sinon.mock(otherContract.methods);

  mock.expects("otherFunction").once();

  // Call MyContract's function that calls OtherContract's function

  await myContract.myFunction();

  // Verify that OtherContract's function was called

  mock.verify();

});

});
```

Write a web app that allows the user to interact with a contract using a form.

```html
<!-- Display a form for the user to input data -->

<form id="form">

<label for="input">Input:</label>

<input type="text" id="input" />

<button type="submit">Submit</button>

</form>

<!-- Display the result of the contract function -->

<div id="result"></div>

<script>

// Connect to the Ethereum network and the deployed contract

const web3 = new Web3("https://mainnet.infura.io");

const contractAddress = "0x123...";

const contract = new web3.eth.Contract(abi, contractAddress);

// Listen for form submissions
```

```
document.getElementById("form").addEventListener("submit", e => {
  e.preventDefault();
  // Get the user's input
  const input = document.getElementById("input").value;
  // Call the contract function
  contract.methods.myFunction(input).send((error, result) => {
    document.getElementById("result").innerHTML = result;
  });
});
</script>
```

DEPLOYING CONTRACTS TO THE ETHEREUM MAINNET WITH TRUFFLE

In this chapter, we will look at how to use Truffle to deploy your smart contracts to the Ethereum mainnet. We will cover the following topics:

- Setting up an Ethereum wallet
- Obtaining Ether for deployment
- Deploying contracts to the mainnet with Truffle

By the end of this chapter, you will be able to deploy your contracts to the Ethereum mainnet with Truffle.

Setting Up an Ethereum Wallet

Before you can deploy your contracts to the Ethereum mainnet, you need an Ethereum wallet that contains Ether, the native cryptocurrency of the Ethereum network. There are several options for creating an Ethereum wallet, including:

- MyEtherWallet: A client-side wallet that allows you to create and manage your own Ethereum wallet.
- MetaMask: A browser extension that allows you to manage your Ethereum wallet from your browser.
- Ledger Nano: A hardware wallet that allows you to securely store your Ethereum wallet on a physical device.

Once you have chosen a wallet, follow the instructions to create an Ethereum wallet and secure it with a strong password. Make sure to keep your password and any recovery phrases or keys in a safe place, as you will need them to access your wallet.

Obtaining Ether for Deployment

To deploy your contracts to the Ethereum mainnet, you need Ether to pay for the gas fees of your transactions. There are several ways to obtain Ether, including:

- Buying Ether from an exchange: You can buy Ether from an exchange like Coinbase or Kraken with a credit card or bank transfer.
- Accepting Ether as payment: You can accept Ether as payment for goods or services by providing your Ethereum address as a payment option.
- Earning Ether through mining: You can earn Ether by participating in the process of

validating and adding new transactions to the Ethereum blockchain, known as mining. However, mining requires specialized hardware and can be competitive, so it may not be the most practical option for obtaining Ether for deployment.

Deploying Contracts to the Mainnet with Truffle

To deploy your contracts to the Ethereum mainnet with Truffle, you will need to do the following:

1. Set up your Truffle project for deployment by creating a truffle-config.js file and adding the mainnet network configuration.
2. Write a Truffle migration that deploys your contract to the mainnet.
3. Set the environment variable MNEMONIC to your wallet's mnemonic or private key.
4. Run the Truffle migration to deploy your contract to the mainnet.

Let's go through each of these steps in detail.

1. Set Up your Truffle Project for Deployment

To set up your Truffle project for deployment, create a truffle-config.js file in the root of your project and add the following configuration:

```
module.exports = {
  networks: {
    mainnet: {
      host: "mainnet.infura.io",
      port: 443,
      network_id: "1",
      gasPrice: 20000000000 // 20 Gwei
    }
  }
};
```

This configuration tells Truffle to use the Infura API to connect to the Ethereum mainnet and specifies the gas price to use for transactions. You can adjust the gas price based on the current gas prices on the mainnet.

2. Write a Truffle Migration that Deploys your Contract to the Mainnet

Next, you need to write a Truffle migration that deploys your contract to the mainnet. Create a new file in the migrations directory and add the following code:

```
const MyContract = artifacts.require("MyContract");
module.exports = function(deployer) {
  deployer.deploy(MyContract);
};
```

This migration simply deploys your contract to the mainnet using Truffle's deploy() function.

3. Set the Environment Variable MNEMONIC

To sign your transactions with your Ethereum wallet, you need to set the environment variable MNEMONIC to your wallet's mnemonic or private key. On Unix-based systems, you can do this by running the following command:

```
export MNEMONIC="your mnemonic or private key here"
```

On Windows, you can use the following command:

```
set MNEMONIC="your mnemonic or private key here"
```

Make sure to replace your mnemonic or private key here with your actual mnemonic or private key.

4. Run the Truffle Migration to Deploy your Contract to the Mainnet

To run the Truffle migration and deploy your contract to the mainnet, run the following command:

```
truffle migrate --network mainnet
```

This will deploy your contract to the Ethereum mainnet and output the contract's address. You can then use Truffle or web3.js to interact with your deployed contract.

Conclusion

In this chapter, we learned how to use Truffle to deploy our smart contracts to the Ethereum mainnet. We covered how to set up an Ethereum wallet, obtain Ether for deployment, and use Truffle to deploy our contracts to the mainnet. By following these steps, you can deploy your contracts to the Ethereum mainnet and make them available to anyone on the network.

If you have any questions or need further assistance, you can refer to the Truffle documentation (https://truffleframework.com/docs/) or ask for help in the Truffle community (https://truffleframework.com/community). Happy coding!

Exercises

To review these concepts, we will go through a series of exercises designed to test your understanding and apply what you have learned.

Deploy a contract to the mainnet that stores a value and allows you to update the value.
Write a Truffle migration that deploys a contract and sets an initial value for a contract variable.
Write a web3.js script that connects to a deployed contract and reads the value of a contract variable.
Write a Truffle migration that deploys a contract and calls a contract function to set the value of a contract variable.
Write a Truffle test that checks if a contract function updates the value of a contract variable correctly.

Solutions

Deploy a contract to the mainnet that stores a value and allows you to update the value.

```
pragma solidity ^0.5.0;
```

```
contract MyContract {
 uint public myValue;
 function setMyValue(uint _myValue) public {
  myValue = _myValue;
 }
}
```

To deploy this contract to the mainnet with Truffle, you can use the following migration:

```
const MyContract = artifacts.require("MyContract");
module.exports = function(deployer) {
 deployer.deploy(MyContract);
};
```

Write a Truffle migration that deploys a contract and sets an initial value for a contract variable.

```
const MyContract = artifacts.require("MyContract");
module.exports = function(deployer) {
 deployer.deploy(MyContract, 100).then(() => {
  console.log(`Contract deployed at address: ${MyContract.address}`);
 });
};
```

This migration deploys the contract and sets the value of the myValue contract variable to 100.

Write a web3.js script that connects to a deployed contract and reads the value of a contract variable.

```
const MyContract = require("../build/contracts/MyContract.json");
// Connect to the deployed contract
const contract = new web3.eth.Contract(MyContract.abi, "0x123...");
// Read the value of the contract variable
contract.methods.myValue().call((error, result) => {
 console.log(result);
});
```

This script connects to the deployed contract at the specified address and calls the myValue()function to read the value of the myValue contract variable.

Write a Truffle migration that deploys a contract and calls a contract function to set the value of a contract variable.

```
const MyContract = artifacts.require("MyContract");
module.exports = function(deployer) {
 deployer.deploy(MyContract).then(() => {
```

```
  return MyContract.deployed().then(instance => {
    instance.setMyValue(100);
  });
  });
};
```

This migration deploys the contract and then calls the setMyValue() function to set the value of the myValue contract variable to 100.

Write a Truffle test that checks if a contract function updates the value of a contract variable correctly.

```
const MyContract = artifacts.require("MyContract");
contract("MyContract", () => {
  it("should update the value of the contract variable", async () => {
    const instance = await MyContract.deployed();
    await instance.setMyValue(100);
    const value = await instance.myValue();
    assert.equal(value, 100, "The value of the contract variable was not updated correctly");
  });
});
```

This test deploys the contract, calls the setMyValue() function to set the value of the myValuecontract variable to 100, and then checks if the value was updated correctly using Truffle's assert.equal() function.

MIGRATING CONTRACTS WITH TRUFFLE

As your Ethereum project grows, you may need to update your smart contracts and deploy them to the Ethereum network. This process, known as contract migration, can be complex and time-consuming, especially if you have multiple contracts that depend on each other.

To simplify contract migration, Truffle provides a migration system that allows you to deploy your contracts in a structured and organized way. In this chapter, we will learn how to use Truffle's migration system to deploy and update our smart contracts.

Setting Up Truffle's Migration System

Truffle's migration system is based on a series of files called "migrations" that are located in the migrations directory of your Truffle project. Each migration file contains JavaScript code that deploys or updates your smart contracts.

To set up Truffle's migration system, you need to create a migrations directory in the root of your Truffle project and add a 1_initial_migration.js file with the following code:

```
const Migrations = artifacts.require("Migrations");
module.exports = function(deployer) {
  deployer.deploy(Migrations);
};
```

This migration deploys the Migrations contract, which is a special contract provided by Truffle that keeps track of your project's contract migrations.

Writing a Contract Migration

To write a contract migration, you need to create a new file in the migrations directory with a name that reflects the order in which the migration should be run. For example, if you want to create a migration that runs before the 2_deploy_contracts.js migration, you can name it 1_deploy_dependencies.js.

In the migration file, you can use the deployer object provided by Truffle to deploy your contracts and call contract functions. For example, the following migration deploys a contract and calls a function to set an initial value for a contract variable:

```
const MyContract = artifacts.require("MyContract");
```

```
module.exports = function(deployer) {
  deployer.deploy(MyContract).then(() => {
    return MyContract.deployed().then(instance => {
      instance.setMyValue(100);
    });
  });
};
```

To deploy your contracts and run your migrations, you can use the truffle migrate command. By default, Truffle will run all the migrations in the migrations directory, but you can also specify a specific migration to run using the --to flag:

```
# Run all migrations
truffle migrate
# Run a specific migration
truffle migrate --to 2
```

Migrating Existing Contracts

If you have already deployed your contracts to the Ethereum network, you may need to update them with new code or data. To do this, you can use Truffle's migration system to create a new migration that updates your existing contracts.

For example, the following migration updates the code of an existing contract:

```
const MyContract = artifacts.require("MyContract");
module.exports = function(deployer) {
  deployer.then(async () => {
    const currentContract = await MyContract.deployed();
    const newContract = await MyContract.new();
    await newContract.transferOwnership(currentContract.address);
  });
};
```

This migration first retrieves the deployed instance of the MyContract contract and then deploys a new instance of the contract with the updated code. It then uses the transferOwnership() function to transfer ownership of the new contract to the old contract.

To update the data of an existing contract, you can use the contract's functions to modify the data. For example, the following migration updates the value of a contract variable:

```
const MyContract = artifacts.require("MyContract");
module.exports = function(deployer) {
  deployer.then(async () => {
```

```
const contract = await MyContract.deployed();
await contract.setMyValue(100);
});
};
```

This migration retrieves the deployed instance of the MyContract contract and then calls the setMyValue()function to update the value of the myValue contract variable.

It's important to note that updating the code or data of an existing contract may require you to pay gas fees. Make sure you have enough Ether in your Ethereum wallet to cover the cost of the transaction.

Migrating Contract Dependencies

In some cases, you may have multiple contracts that depend on each other and need to be deployed in a specific order. Truffle's migration system allows you to specify the order in which your migrations should be run using the naming conventions we discussed earlier.

For example, if your MyContract contract depends on the MyLibrary contract, you can create a 1_deploy_dependencies.js migration that deploys the MyLibrary contract first, and then a 2_deploy_contracts.js migration that deploys the MyContract contract:

```
// 1_deploy_dependencies.js
const MyLibrary = artifacts.require("MyLibrary");
module.exports = function(deployer) {
  deployer.deploy(MyLibrary);
};
// 2_deploy_contracts.js
const MyContract = artifacts.require("MyContract");
module.exports = function(deployer) {
  deployer.deploy(MyContract);
};
```

When you run the truffle migrate command, Truffle will automatically run the migrations in the correct order, ensuring that the dependencies of your contracts are deployed first.

Conclusion

In this chapter, we learned how to use Truffle's migration system to deploy and update our smart contracts. We covered how to set up Truffle's migration system, how to write contract migrations, how to migrate existing contracts, and how to migrate contract dependencies.

Using Truffle's migration system, you can deploy and update your contracts in a structured and organized way, simplifying the process of working with Ethereum. In the next chapter, we will learn how to use Truffle's built-in testing tools to test our contracts and ensure that they are working as expected.

If you have any questions or need further assistance, you can refer to the Truffle documentation (https://truffleframework.com/docs/) or ask for help in the Truffle community (https://truffleframework.com/community). Happy coding!

Exercises

To review these concepts, we will go through a series of exercises designed to test your understanding and apply what you have learned.

Write a Truffle migration that deploys two contracts, ContractA **and** ContractB, **where** ContractB **depends on** ContractA.

Write a Truffle test that checks if a contract function correctly updates the value of a contract variable.

Write a Truffle migration that updates the code of an existing contract and transfers ownership of the new contract to the old contract.

Write a Truffle migration that updates the value of a contract variable in an existing contract.

Write a Truffle test that checks if a contract function correctly calls another contract function and returns the correct value.

Solutions

Write a Truffle migration that deploys two contracts, ContractA **and** ContractB, **where** ContractB **depends on** ContractA.

```
const ContractA = artifacts.require("ContractA");
const ContractB = artifacts.require("ContractB");
module.exports = function(deployer) {
  deployer.deploy(ContractA).then(() => {
    return deployer.deploy(ContractB, ContractA.address);
  });
};
```

This migration deploys ContractA first and then deploys ContractB, passing the address of ContractAas an argument.

Write a Truffle test that checks if a contract function correctly updates the value of a contract variable.

```
const MyContract = artifacts.require("MyContract");
contract("MyContract", () => {
  it("should update the value of the contract variable", async () => {
    const instance = await MyContract.deployed();
    await instance.setMyValue(100);
    const value = await instance.myValue();
```

```
    assert.equal(value, 100, "The value of the contract variable was not updated correctly");
  });
});
```

This test deploys the contract, calls the setMyValue() function to set the value of the myValuecontract variable to 100, and then checks if the value was updated correctly using Truffle's assert.equal() function.

Write a Truffle migration that updates the code of an existing contract and transfers ownership of the new contract to the old contract.

```
const MyContract = artifacts.require("MyContract");
module.exports = function(deployer) {
  deployer.then(async () => {
    const currentContract = await MyContract.deployed();
    const newContract = await MyContract.new();
    await newContract.transferOwnership(currentContract.address);
  });
};
```

This migration first retrieves the deployed instance of the MyContract contract and then deploys a new instance of the contract with the updated code. It then uses the transferOwnership() function to transfer ownership of the new contract to the old contract.

Write a Truffle migration that updates the value of a contract variable in an existing contract.

```
const MyContract = artifacts.require("MyContract");
module.exports = function(deployer) {
  deployer.then(async () => {
    const contract = await MyContract.deployed();
    await contract.setMyValue(100);
  });
};
```

This migration retrieves the deployed instance of the MyContract contract and then calls the setMyValue() function to update the value of the myValue contract variable.

Write a Truffle test that checks if a contract function correctly calls another contract function and returns the correct value.

```
const MyContract = artifacts.require("MyContract");
const OtherContract = artifacts.require("OtherContract");
contract("MyContract", () => {
  it("should call another contract function and return the correct value", async () => {
    const instance = await MyContract.deployed();
```

```
    const otherInstance = await OtherContract.deployed();
    await otherInstance.setMyValue(100);
    const value = await instance.getOtherValue();
    assert.equal(value, 100, "The value returned from the other contract was not correct");
  });
});
```

This test deploys both the MyContract and OtherContract contracts, sets the value of a contract variable in the OtherContract contract, and then calls the getOtherValue() function in the MyContract contract to retrieve the value. It then uses Truffle's assert.equal() function to compare the returned value to the expected value.

USING TRUFFLE'S BUILT-IN SECURITY TOOLS

As a blockchain developer, security is a critical aspect of your work. It's important to ensure that your contracts are free of vulnerabilities and that your code is safe and secure. In this chapter, we will learn how to use Truffle's built-in security tools to help ensure the security of your contracts.

Truffle's Static Analysis Tools

Truffle includes several static analysis tools that you can use to analyze your contract code for potential vulnerabilities. These tools include:

- Mythril: a security analysis tool that uses symbolic execution to find vulnerabilities in Ethereum smart contracts
- Oyente: a security analysis tool that uses symbolic execution to find vulnerabilities in Ethereum smart contracts
- Solium: a linter for Solidity code that checks for style and security issues

To use these tools, you can install them using npm and then run them on your contract code:

```
$ npm install -g mythril oyente solium
```
```
$ mythril my_contract.sol
```
```
$ oyente my_contract.sol
```
```
$ solium -f my_contract.sol
```

These tools will analyze your contract code and report any potential vulnerabilities or issues that they find. It's important to regularly run these tools on your contract code to ensure that it is secure.

Truffle's Testing Tools

In addition to static analysis tools, Truffle also includes several testing tools that you can use to test your contracts for vulnerabilities. These tools include:

- Truffle Assertions: a library of utility functions for testing Solidity contracts
- Truffle Debugger: a debugger for Solidity contracts that allows you to step through your contract code and inspect variables

To use these tools, you can include them in your Truffle tests:

```
const truffleAssert = require("truffle-assertions");
```
```
const TruffleDebugger = require("truffle-debugger");
```

```
contract("MyContract", () => {
  it("should do something securely", async () => {
    const instance = await MyContract.deployed();
    const result = await instance.doSomething();
    truffleAssert.eventEmitted(result, "SomethingDone");
    TruffleDebugger.watch(instance);
  });
});
```

The truffleAssert library provides a variety of utility functions that you can use to test your contracts, such as eventEmitted(), which checks if a specific event was emitted by the contract. The TruffleDebugger allows you to step through your contract code and inspect variables to ensure that it is working as expected.

Using Truffle's Security Best Practices

In addition to Truffle's built-in security tools, there are several best practices that you can follow to ensure the security of your contracts. Some of these best practices include:

- Writing tests for all of your contract functions to ensure that they are working as expected
- Regularly running static analysis tools on your contract code to identify potential vulnerabilities
- Using the Truffle Debugger to step through your contract code and inspect variables
- Following Solidity best practices, such as using the require() function to ensure that input values are valid and using the view and pure functions to mark functions that do not modify contract state

By following these best practices, you can help ensure that your contracts are secure and free of vulnerabilities.

Conclusion

In this chapter, we learned about Truffle's built-in security tools and best practices for ensuring the security of your contracts. We covered Truffle's static analysis tools and testing tools, as well as best practices for writing secure contract code. By using these tools and following these best practices, you can help ensure the security of your contracts and protect against potential vulnerabilities.

If you have any questions or need further assistance, you can refer to the Truffle documentation (https://truffleframework.com/docs/) or ask for help in the Truffle community (https://truffleframework.com/community). Happy coding!

Exercises

To review these concepts, we will go through a series of exercises designed to test your understanding and apply what you have learned.

Install Mythril, Oyente, and Solium using npm and run them on a Solidity contract file.

Write a Truffle test that uses the truffleAssert library to check if a specific event was emitted by a contract.

Use the Truffle Debugger to step through a contract function and inspect variables.

Follow Solidity best practices by using the require() function to ensure that input values are valid and using the view and pure functions to mark functions that do not modify contract state.

Use Truffle's built-in security tools and best practices to secure a contract that manages a simple token.

Solutions

Install Mythril, Oyente, and Solium using npm and run them on a Solidity contract file.

```
$ npm install -g mythril oyente solium
```
```
$ mythril my_contract.sol
```
```
$ oyente my_contract.sol
```
```
$ solium -f my_contract.sol
```

Write a Truffle test that uses the truffleAssert library to check if a specific event was emitted by a contract.

```
const truffleAssert = require("truffle-assertions");
contract("MyContract", () => {
 it("should emit a specific event", async () => {
  const instance = await MyContract.deployed();
  const result = await instance.doSomething();
  truffleAssert.eventEmitted(result, "SomethingDone");
 });
});
```

This test deploys the MyContract contract and calls the doSomething() function. It then uses the eventEmitted() function from the truffleAssert library to check if the SomethingDone event was emitted by the contract.

Use the Truffle Debugger to step through a contract function and inspect variables.

```
const TruffleDebugger = require("truffle-debugger");
contract("MyContract", () => {
 it("should debug a contract function", async () => {
  const instance = await MyContract.deployed();
  TruffleDebugger.watch(instance);
  await instance.doSomething();
 });
});
```

This test deploys the MyContract contract and uses the TruffleDebugger.watch() function to enable the debugger for the contract. It then calls the doSomething() function, which will allow you to step through the function and inspect variables using the Truffle Debugger.

Follow Solidity best practices by using the require() **function to ensure that input values are valid and using the** view **and** pure **functions to mark functions that do not modify contract state.**

```solidity
pragma solidity ^0.6.0;
contract MyContract {
  uint public myValue;
  function setMyValue(uint _value) public {
    require(_value > 0, "Value must be greater than 0");
    myValue = _value;
  }
  function getMyValue() public view returns (uint) {
    return myValue;
  }
  function incrementMyValue() public pure {
    myValue++;
  }
}
```

In this contract, the setMyValue() function uses the require() function to ensure that the input value is greater than 0. The getMyValue() function is marked with the view modifier, indicating that it does not modify contract state. The incrementMyValue() function is marked with the pure modifier, indicating that it does not modify contract state or access external resources.

Use Truffle's built-in security tools and best practices to secure a contract that manages a simple token.

Here are some steps you can follow to secure a simple token contract using Truffle's built-in security tools and best practices:

1. Write tests for all of the contract's functions to ensure that they are working as expected.
2. Run static analysis tools on the contract code to identify potential vulnerabilities.
3. Use the Truffle Debugger to step through the contract functions and inspect variables.
4. Follow Solidity best practices, such as using the require() function to ensure that input values are valid and using the view and pure functions to mark functions that do not modify contract state.
5. Regularly run the static analysis tools and tests on the contract to ensure its continued security.

USING TRUFFLE WITH OTHER ETHEREUM DEVELOPMENT TOOLS (E.G. REMIX, METAMASK)

In this chapter, we will learn how to use Truffle with other Ethereum development tools such as Remix and MetaMask. These tools can be used in conjunction with Truffle to enhance your Ethereum development workflow and provide additional functionality.

Remix

Remix is a browser-based Solidity compiler and runtime environment. It allows you to write, compile, and deploy Solidity contracts directly in your web browser. Remix also includes a debugger and testing tools, making it a powerful tool for Ethereum development.

To use Remix with Truffle, you can simply copy and paste your Solidity contract code into Remix. You can then compile and deploy your contract using Remix's user interface.

```
pragma solidity ^0.6.0;
contract MyContract {
 uint public myValue;
 function setMyValue(uint _value) public {
  myValue = _value;
 }
 function getMyValue() public view returns (uint) {
  return myValue;
 }
}
```

MetaMask

MetaMask is a browser extension that allows you to interact with the Ethereum blockchain from your web browser. It allows you to manage your Ethereum accounts, send and receive transactions, and interact with dApps.

To use MetaMask with Truffle, you can simply connect your MetaMask account to your Truffle project. This allows you to deploy and interact with your Truffle contracts using MetaMask.

Conclusion

In this chapter, we learned how to use Truffle with other Ethereum development tools such as Remix and MetaMask. These tools can be used in conjunction with Truffle to enhance your Ethereum development workflow and provide additional functionality. By using Truffle with these tools, you can streamline your Ethereum development process and build powerful dApps.

If you have any questions or need further assistance, you can refer to the Truffle documentation (https://truffleframework.com/docs/) or ask for help in the Truffle community (https://truffleframework.com/community). Happy coding!

Exercises

To review these concepts, we will go through a series of exercises designed to test your understanding and apply what you have learned.

Connect your MetaMask account to a Truffle project.
Deploy a Truffle contract using MetaMask.
Interact with a Truffle contract using MetaMask.
Use Remix's debugger to debug a Solidity contract.
Use Remix's testing tools to write and run tests for a Solidity contract.

Solutions

Connect your MetaMask account to a Truffle project.
To do this, first make sure that you have the MetaMask extension installed in your web browser. Then, open your Truffle project in your code editor and import the web3 library. You can then use the Web3.givenProvider property to connect to your MetaMask account:

```
const Web3 = require("web3");
const web3 = new Web3(Web3.givenProvider);
```

Deploy a Truffle contract using MetaMask.
To do this, first make sure that you have connected your MetaMask account to your Truffle project as described in the previous exercise. Then, you can use Truffle's deploy() function to deploy your contract to the Ethereum network:

```
const MyContract = artifacts.require("MyContract");
module.exports = async function(deployer) {
  await deployer.deploy(MyContract);
};
```

Interact with a Truffle contract using MetaMask.
To do this, first make sure that you have deployed your Truffle contract to the Ethereum network using MetaMask. Then, you can use Truffle's at() function to get an instance of the contract and call its functions:

```
const MyContract = artifacts.require("MyContract");
module.exports = async function(callback) {
  const instance = await MyContract.at(contractAddress);
  const result = await instance.doSomething();
  console.log(result);
};
```

Use Remix's debugger to debug a Solidity contract.

To do this, first copy and paste your Solidity contract code into Remix. Then, click the "Debug" button to open the debugger. You can then use the debugger's user interface to step through your contract code and inspect variables.

Use Remix's testing tools to write and run tests for a Solidity contract.

To do this, first copy and paste your Solidity contract code into Remix. Then, click the "Test" button to open the testing tools. You can then write and run tests for your contract using Remix's user interface. You can also use the assert() function to check the results of your tests:

```
it("should do something", async () => {
  const result = await MyContract.doSomething();
  assert.equal(result, expectedResult, "Unexpected result");
});
```

A WALKTHROUGH OF THE DAPP DEVELOPMENT PROCESS WITH TRUFFLE

In this chapter, we will walk through the process of developing a decentralized application (DApp) using Truffle. We will cover the entire process from start to finish, including writing and testing smart contracts, building a user interface, and deploying the DApp to the Ethereum mainnet.

Step 1: Write and Test Smart Contracts

The first step in developing a DApp is to write and test your smart contracts. Smart contracts are the foundation of any DApp, as they define the business logic and rules of the application.

To write and test smart contracts with Truffle, you can follow these steps:

1. Write your Solidity contract code.
2. Compile your contracts using Truffle's compile command.
3. Write tests for your contracts using Truffle's testing framework.
4. Run the tests using Truffle's test command.

Here is an example of a simple Solidity contract and its corresponding test file:

```solidity
pragma solidity ^0.6.0;
contract MyContract {
 uint public myValue;
 function setMyValue(uint _value) public {
  myValue = _value;
 }
 function getMyValue() public view returns (uint) {
  return myValue;
 }
}
const MyContract = artifacts.require("MyContract");
contract("MyContract", () => {
 it("should set and get a value", async () => {
  const instance = await MyContract.deployed();
```

```
await instance.setMyValue(123);
const value = await instance.getMyValue();
assert.equal(value, 123, "Unexpected value");
});
});
```

Step 2: Build a User Interface

The next step in developing a DApp is to build a user interface (UI) for it. The UI is what users will interact with to use your DApp.

To build a UI for a DApp with Truffle, you can follow these steps:

1. Choose a frontend framework such as React or Angular.
2. Set up a new project using the chosen framework.
3. Install web3.js, the JavaScript library for interacting with the Ethereum blockchain.
4. Connect to the Ethereum network and your contract using web3.js.
5. Write UI code to call your contract's functions and display the results to the user.

Here is an example of a simple React component that calls a contract function and displays the result:

```
import React, { useEffect, useState } from "react";
import Web3 from "web3";
const MyComponent = () => {
  const [value, setValue] = useState(null);
  useEffect(() => {
    async function fetchData() {
      const web3 = new Web3(Web3.givenProvider || "http://localhost:8545");
      const contract = new web3.eth.Contract(ABI, contractAddress);
      const result = await contract.methods.getMyValue().call();
      setValue(result);
    }
    fetchData();
  }, []);
  return <div>{value}</div>;
};
```

In this example, we first import the useEffect and useState hooks from React. We then define a state variable called value and a function called setValue to update it.

Next, we use the useEffect hook to fetch data from our contract when the component mounts. We do this by creating an async function called fetchData and calling it inside the useEffect hook.

Inside fetchData, we first create an instance of the Web3 library and pass it the Ethereum provider from MetaMask. We then create an instance of our contract using the Web3 library and the contract's ABI (Application Binary Interface) and address.

Finally, we call the contract's getMyValue function using the call method and set the result to the valuestate variable using the setValue function.

Step 3: Deploy the DApp to the Ethereum Mainnet

The final step in developing a DApp is to deploy it to the Ethereum mainnet. This makes the DApp accessible to anyone with an internet connection and an Ethereum wallet.

To deploy a DApp to the Ethereum mainnet with Truffle, you can follow these steps:

1. Set up an account on a cryptocurrency exchange such as Coinbase or Binance.
2. Buy some Ethereum using the exchange.
3. Set up a wallet such as MetaMask to hold and manage your Ethereum.
4. Configure Truffle to use the Ethereum mainnet.
5. Run Truffle's migrate command to deploy your contracts to the mainnet.

Once your DApp is deployed, users will be able to access it using their Ethereum wallet and interact with your contracts using the UI you built.

Conclusion

In this chapter, we covered the process of developing a DApp using Truffle from start to finish. We wrote and tested smart contracts, built a UI, and deployed the DApp to the Ethereum mainnet. With these skills, you are now equipped to create your own DApps using Truffle.

However, keep in mind that developing DApps is a complex process and there is much more to learn beyond what we covered in this course. If you want to dive deeper into DApp development, we recommend exploring additional resources such as the Truffle documentation and online tutorials.

If you have any questions or need further assistance, you can refer to the Truffle documentation (https://truffleframework.com/docs/) or ask for help in the Truffle community (https://truffleframework.com/community). Happy coding!

Exercises

To review these concepts, we will go through a series of exercises designed to test your understanding and apply what you have learned.

Create a new Solidity contract called "MyCounter" that has a public variable called "count" initialized to 0. Add two public functions, "increment" and "decrement" that respectively increase and decrease the value of "count" by 1.
Write a test file that deploys an instance of "MyCounter" and calls the "increment" and "decrement" functions to ensure they are working as expected.
Create a new React app using the create-react-app tool.
Install web3.js and connect to the Ethereum mainnet using your MetaMask provider.
Create a new component called "MyCounter" that displays the current value of "count" from the

"MyCounter" contract and has buttons to increment and decrement the value.

Deploy the "MyCounter" contract to the Ethereum mainnet using Truffle.

Update the "MyCounter" component to connect to the deployed contract and call its functions instead of using a test contract.

Add a form to the "MyCounter" component that allows users to input a custom value to increment or decrement the count by.

Update the "increment" and "decrement" functions to accept a value parameter and add/subtract that amount from the count.

Add a function to the "MyCounter" contract called "reset" that sets the count back to 0.

Add a button to the "MyCounter" component that calls the "reset" function when clicked.

Test the "reset" function by manually setting the count to a non-zero value and then resetting it.

Solutions

Create a new Solidity contract called "MyCounter" that has a public variable called "count" initialized to 0. Add two public functions, "increment" and "decrement" that respectively increase and decrease the value of "count" by 1.

Write a test file that deploys an instance of "MyCounter" and calls the "increment" and "decrement" functions to ensure they are working as expected.

Here is the Solidity code for the "MyCounter" contract:

```solidity
pragma solidity ^0.7.0;
contract MyCounter {
 uint public count = 0;
 function increment() public {
  count++;
 }
 function decrement() public {
  count--;
 }
}
```

And here is the test file:

```javascript
const MyCounter = artifacts.require("MyCounter");
contract("MyCounter", () => {
 it("should increment and decrement the count correctly", async () => {
  const myCounter = await MyCounter.new();
  await myCounter.increment();
  const count = await myCounter.count();
  assert.equal(count, 1, "count should be 1 after incrementing");
  await myCounter.decrement();
```

```
  const count2 = await myCounter.count();

  assert.equal(count2, 0, "count should be 0 after decrementing");

});

});
```

Create a new React app using the create-react-app tool.
Install web3.js and connect to the Ethereum mainnet using your MetaMask provider.
Create a new component called "MyCounter" that displays the current value of "count" from the "MyCounter" contract and has buttons to increment and decrement the value.

To create a new React app, run the following command:

```
npx create-react-app my-app
```

Then, install web3.js by running:

```
cd my-app
```

```
npm install web3
```

Here is the code for the "MyCounter" component:

```
import React, { useEffect, useState } from "react";

import Web3 from "web3";

const MyCounter = () => {

  const [count, setCount] = useState(null);

  useEffect(() => {

   async function fetchData() {

    const web3 = new Web3(Web3.givenProvider || "http://localhost:8545");

    const contract = new web3.eth.Contract(ABI, contractAddress);

    const count = await contract.methods.count().call();

    setCount(count);

   }

   fetchData();

  }, []);

  const increment = async () => {

   const web3 = new Web3(Web3.givenProvider || "http://localhost:8545");

   const contract = new web3.eth.Contract(ABI, contractAddress);

   await contract.methods.increment().send({ from: web3.eth.defaultAccount });

   const count = await contract.methods.count().call();

   setCount(count);

  };

  const decrement = async () => {
```

```
const web3 = new Web3(Web3.givenProvider || "http://localhost:8545");
const contract = new web3.eth.Contract(ABI, contractAddress);
await contract.methods.decrement().send({ from: web3.eth.defaultAccount });
const count = await contract.methods.count().call();
setCount(count);
};
return (
<div>
  <div>Count: {count}</div>
  <button onClick={increment}>Increment</button>
  <button onClick={decrement}>Decrement</button>
</div>
);
};
```

Deploy the "MyCounter" contract to the Ethereum mainnet using Truffle.
Update the "MyCounter" component to connect to the deployed contract and call its functions instead of using a test contract.
To deploy the "MyCounter" contract to the Ethereum mainnet, first set up a configuration file for Truffle. Inside the truffle-config.js file, add the following:

```
const HDWalletProvider = require("@truffle/hdwallet-provider");
module.exports = {
networks: {
 mainnet: {
  provider: () =>
   new HDWalletProvider(
    process.env.MNEMONIC,
     `https://mainnet.infura.io/v3/${process.env.INFURA_API_KEY}`
   ),
   network_id: 1,
   gas: 7000000,
   gasPrice: 1000000000,
  },
 },
};
```

Replace process.env.MNEMONIC with your mnemonic and process.env.INFURA_API_KEY with your Infura API key.

Next, run the following command to compile and migrate the contract to the mainnet:

```
truffle migrate --network mainnet
```

Make sure you have enough Ether in your account to pay for the gas fees.

Add a form to the "MyCounter" component that allows users to input a custom value to increment or decrement the count by.
Update the "increment" and "decrement" functions to accept a value parameter and add/subtract that amount from the count.

Here is the updated "MyCounter" component with a form to input a custom value to increment or decrement the count by:

```javascript
import React, { useEffect, useState } from "react";
import Web3 from "web3";
const MyCounter = () => {
  const [count, setCount] = useState(null);
  const [value, setValue] = useState(0);
  useEffect(() => {
    async function fetchData() {
      const web3 = new Web3(Web3.givenProvider || "http://localhost:8545");
      const contract = new web3.eth.Contract(ABI, contractAddress);
      const count = await contract.methods.count().call();
      setCount(count);
    }
    fetchData();
  }, []);
  const increment = async () => {
    const web3 = new Web3(Web3.givenProvider || "http://localhost:8545");
    const contract = new web3.eth.Contract(ABI, contractAddress);
    await contract.methods.increment(value).send({ from: web3.eth.defaultAccount });
    const count = await contract.methods.count().call();
    setCount(count);
  };
  const decrement = async () => {
    const web3 = new Web3(Web3.givenProvider || "http://localhost:8545");
    const contract = new web3.eth.Contract(ABI, contractAddress);
    await contract.methods.decrement(value).send({ from: web3.eth.defaultAccount });
    const count = await contract.methods.count().call();
    setCount(count);
```

```
};
return (
<div>
 <div>Count: {count}</div>
 <form>
  <label>
   Value:
   <input type="number" value={value} onChange={(event) => setValue(event.target.value)} />
  </label>
 </form>
 <button onClick={increment}>Increment</button>
 <button onClick={decrement}>Decrement</button>
</div>
);
};
```

Add a function to the "MyCounter" contract called "reset" that sets the count back to 0.
Add a button to the "MyCounter" component that calls the "reset" function when clicked.
Test the "reset" function by manually setting the count to a non-zero value and then resetting it.
Here is an example of a "MyCounter" contract that allows the owner to set the count to a custom value:

```
pragma solidity ^0.7.0;
contract MyCounter {
 uint public count = 0;
 constructor() public {
  count = 100;
 }
 function setCount(uint _count) public {
  require(msg.sender == owner, "Only the owner can set the count.");
  count = _count;
 }
}
```

To set the count to a custom value, call the setCount function and pass in the desired value as an argument. For example:

```
const web3 = new Web3(Web3.givenProvider || "http://localhost:8545");
const contract = new web3.eth.Contract(ABI, contractAddress);
await contract.methods.setCount(50).send({ from: web3.eth.defaultAccount });
```

TIPS AND BEST PRACTICES FOR BUILDING DAPPS WITH TRUFFLE

Tips and Best Practices for Building DApps with Truffle

Learn Truffle Tips and Best Practices for Building DApps with Truffle

IN PROGRESS

Truffle is a popular development framework for building decentralized applications (DApps) on the Ethereum blockchain. As you start building your own DApps with Truffle, here are some tips and best practices to keep in mind:

Use the Latest Version of Truffle

As with any software, it's important to keep your Truffle version up to date. New versions of Truffle often include bug fixes, performance improvements, and new features. To update Truffle, run the following command:

```
npm update -g truffle
```

Follow Solidity Best Practices

Solidity is the programming language used to write Ethereum smart contracts. When writing Solidity code, it's important to follow best practices to ensure the security and reliability of your contracts. Here are some tips:

- Use the latest version of Solidity. As with Truffle, new versions of Solidity often include bug fixes and improvements.
- Use explicit visibility (i.e. public, internal, private) for all functions and variables. This helps prevent accidental contract breaches and improves code readability.
- Use the assert and require functions to validate input and enforce invariants.
- Use the view and pure functions to mark functions that do not modify contract state. This can improve contract performance and reduce gas costs.

Test Your Contracts Thoroughly

Testing is an important part of the development process, and it's especially important when building DApps on the blockchain. Truffle provides a powerful testing framework that makes it easy to write and run tests for your contracts. Some best practices for testing your contracts include:

- Write tests for all functions in your contracts. This includes both positive and negative

test cases.
- Use Truffle's utility functions (e.g. web3.eth.getBalance, web3.eth.getTransactionReceipt) to inspect the state of your contracts and the Ethereum network during tests.
- Use the Truffle Debugger to debug failing tests and understand what went wrong.

Use a Version Control System

As with any software project, it's important to use a version control system (e.g. Git) to track changes to your code. This helps you revert to previous versions if something goes wrong, and it makes it easier to collaborate with other developers.

Use a Linter

A linter is a tool that helps you enforce coding style and catch syntax errors in your code. For Solidity, we recommend using the Solidity Linter. To install it, run the following command:

```
npm install -g solium
```

Then, you can run solium from the command line to lint your Solidity code. For example:

```
solium -d contracts/
```

This will lint all Solidity files in the contracts/ directory.

Use a Security Audit Tool

Security is critical when building DApps on the blockchain. To ensure the security of your contracts, we recommend using a security audit tool like Mythril or Oyente. These tools can help you identify potential vulnerabilities in your contracts, such as reentrancy attacks or uninitialized storage variables.

Conclusion

By following these tips and best practices, you can build high-quality DApps with Truffle that are reliable, secure, and scalable. With a little effort and attention to detail, you can create DApps that are ready for deployment on the Ethereum mainnet.

As you continue to build DApps with Truffle, keep an eye out for new best practices and tools that can help you improve your workflow and code quality. With the right tools and techniques, building DApps with Truffle can be a fun and rewarding experience.

If you have any questions or need further assistance, you can refer to the Truffle documentation (https://truffleframework.com/docs/) or ask for help in the Truffle community (https://truffleframework.com/community). Happy coding!

Exercises

To review these concepts, we will go through a series of exercises designed to test your understanding and apply what you have learned.

Write a Solidity contract that defines a "Bank" contract with the following functionality:

-The contract has an owner and a balance.

-The owner can deposit ether into the contract by calling the deposit function.

-The owner can withdraw ether from the contract by calling the withdraw function.

-The contract has a transfer function that allows the owner to send ether to another address.

-The contract has a kill function that allows the owner to destroy the contract and withdraw all remaining balance.

Write a Truffle test for the Bank contract from Exercise 1 that does the following:

-Deploys a new instance of the Bank contract.

-Calls the deposit function to deposit 1 ether into the contract.

-Calls the withdraw function to withdraw 0.5 ether from the contract.

-Calls the transfer function to send 0.25 ether to another address.

-Calls the kill function to destroy the contract and withdraw the remaining balance.

Write a Solidity contract that defines a "Voting" contract with the following functionality:

-The contract has a list of candidates, represented as strings.

-The contract has a function that allows a voter to cast a vote for a specific candidate.

-The contract has a function that returns the number of votes received by each candidate.

-The contract has a function that allows the owner to add new candidates to the list.

Write a Truffle test for the Voting contract from Exercise 3 that does the following:

-Deploys a new instance of the Voting contract with 3 candidates (Alice, Bob, and Charlie).

-Calls the vote function twice to cast votes for Alice and Bob.

-Calls the getVotes function to retrieve the vote count for each candidate.

-Asserts that Alice has 1 vote and Bob has 1 vote.

-Calls the addCandidate function to add a new candidate (Dave).

-Calls the vote function to cast a vote for Dave.

-Calls the getVotes function to retrieve the vote count for each candidate.

-Asserts that Dave has 1 vote.

Write a Solidity contract that defines a "Token" contract with the following functionality:

-The contract has a name, symbol, and total supply.

-The contract has a function that allows the owner to mint new tokens and add them to their balance.

-The contract has a function that allows a user to transfer tokens to another address.

-The contract has a function that returns the balance of a specific address.

Solutions

Write a Solidity contract that defines a "Bank" contract with the following functionality:

-The contract has an owner and a balance.

-The owner can deposit ether into the contract by calling the deposit function.

-The owner can withdraw ether from the contract by calling the withdraw function.

-The contract has a transfer function that allows the owner to send ether to another address.

-The contract has a kill function that allows the owner to destroy the contract and withdraw all remaining balance.

```solidity
pragma solidity ^0.6.0;

contract Bank {
    address public owner;
```

```solidity
uint public balance;
constructor() public {
    owner = msg.sender;
}
function deposit() public payable {
    require(msg.value > 0, "Cannot deposit 0 or less ether.");
    balance += msg.value;
}
function withdraw(uint amount) public {
    require(amount <= balance, "Insufficient balance.");
    require(amount > 0, "Cannot withdraw 0 or less ether.");
    balance -= amount;
    msg.sender.transfer(amount);
}
function transfer(address recipient, uint amount) public {
    require(amount <= balance, "Insufficient balance.");
    require(amount > 0, "Cannot transfer 0 or less ether.");
    balance -= amount;
    recipient.transfer(amount);
}
function kill() public {
    require(balance > 0, "Cannot kill contract with 0 balance.");
    owner.transfer(balance);
    selfdestruct(owner);
}
}
```

Write a Truffle test for the Bank **contract from Exercise 1 that does the following:**
-**Deploys a new instance of the** Bank **contract.**
-**Calls the** deposit **function to deposit 1 ether into the contract.**
-**Calls the** withdraw **function to withdraw 0.5 ether from the contract.**
-**Calls the** transfer **function to send 0.25 ether to another address.**
-**Calls the** kill **function to destroy the contract and withdraw the remaining balance.**

```javascript
const Bank = artifacts.require("Bank");
contract("Bank", () => {
    it("should allow the owner to deposit, withdraw, transfer, and kill the contract", async () => {
        const bank = await Bank.new();
        const owner = await bank.owner();
```

```javascript
    const recipient = "0x1234567890abcdef1234567890abcdef12345678";
    // Deposit 1 ether
    await web3.eth.sendTransaction({
      to: bank.address,
      from: owner,
      value: web3.utils.toWei("1", "ether")
    });
    assert.equal((await bank.balance()).toString(), web3.utils.toWei("1", "ether"));
    // Withdraw 0.5 ether
    await bank.withdraw(web3.utils.toWei("0.5", "ether"), { from: owner });
    assert.equal((await bank.balance()).toString(), web3.utils.toWei("0.5", "ether"));
    // Transfer 0.25 ether
    await bank.transfer(recipient, web3.utils.toWei("0.25", "ether"), { from: owner });
    assert.equal((await bank.balance()).toString(), web3.utils.toWei("0.25", "ether"));
    // Kill contract
    const initialBalance = await web3.eth.getBalance(owner);
    await bank.kill({ from: owner });
    assert.equal((await        web3.eth.getBalance(owner)).toString(),
initialBalance.add(web3.utils.toBN(web3.utils.toWei("0.25", "ether"))).toString());
  });
});
```

Write a Solidity contract that defines a "Voting" contract with the following functionality:
-The contract has a list of candidates, represented as strings.
-The contract has a function that allows a voter to cast a vote for a specific candidate.
-The contract has a function that returns the number of votes received by each candidate.
-The contract has a function that allows the owner to add new candidates to the list.

```solidity
pragma solidity ^0.6.0;
import "https://github.com/OpenZeppelin/openzeppelin-solidity/contracts/utils/SafeMath.sol";
contract Bank {
  using SafeMath for uint;
  address public owner;
  mapping(address => uint) public balances;
  uint public totalBalance;
  constructor() public {
    owner = msg.sender;
  }
  function deposit() public payable {
```

```solidity
    require(msg.value > 0, "Cannot deposit 0 or less ether.");
    balances[msg.sender] = balances[msg.sender].add(msg.value);
    totalBalance = totalBalance.add(msg.value);
}
function withdraw(uint amount) public {
    require(amount <= balances[msg.sender], "Insufficient balance.");
    require(amount > 0, "Cannot withdraw 0 or less ether.");
    balances[msg.sender] = balances[msg.sender].sub(amount);
    totalBalance = totalBalance.sub(amount);
    msg.sender.transfer(amount);
}
function transfer(address recipient, uint amount) public {
    require(amount <= balances[msg.sender], "Insufficient balance.");
    require(amount > 0, "Cannot transfer 0 or less ether.");
    balances[msg.sender] = balances[msg.sender].sub(amount);
    balances[recipient] = balances[recipient].add(amount);
}
function kill() public {
    require(totalBalance > 0, "Cannot kill contract with 0 balance.");
    require(msg.sender == owner, "Only the owner can kill the contract.");
    owner.transfer(totalBalance);
    selfdestruct(owner);
}
}
```

Write a Truffle test for the Voting contract from Exercise 3 that does the following:
-Deploys a new instance of the Voting contract with 3 candidates (Alice, Bob, and Charlie).
-Calls the vote function twice to cast votes for Alice and Bob.
-Calls the getVotes function to retrieve the vote count for each candidate.
-Asserts that Alice has 1 vote and Bob has 1 vote.
-Calls the addCandidate function to add a new candidate (Dave).
-Calls the vote function to cast a vote for Dave.
-Calls the getVotes function to retrieve the vote count for each candidate.
-Asserts that Dave has 1 vote.

```solidity
pragma solidity ^0.6.0;
import "https://github.com/OpenZeppelin/openzeppelin-solidity/contracts/utils/SafeMath.sol";
contract Bank {
    using SafeMath for uint;
```

```solidity
address public owner;

mapping(address => uint) public balances;

uint public totalBalance;

constructor() public {

    owner = msg.sender;

}

function deposit() public payable {

    require(msg.value > 0, "Cannot deposit 0 or less ether.");

    balances[msg.sender] = balances[msg.sender].add(msg.value);

    totalBalance = totalBalance.add(msg.value);

}

function withdraw(uint amount) public {

    require(amount <= balances[msg.sender], "Insufficient balance.");

    require(amount > 0, "Cannot withdraw 0 or less ether.");

    balances[msg.sender] = balances[msg.sender].sub(amount);

    totalBalance = totalBalance.sub(amount);

    msg.sender.transfer(amount);

}

function transfer(address recipient, uint amount) public {

    require(amount <= balances[msg.sender], "Insufficient balance.");

    require(amount > 0, "Cannot transfer 0 or less ether.");

    balances[msg.sender] = balances[msg.sender].sub(amount);

    balances[recipient] = balances[recipient].add(amount);

}

function kill() public {

    require(totalBalance > 0, "Cannot kill contract with 0 balance.");

    require(msg.sender == owner, "Only the owner can kill the contract.");

    owner.transfer(totalBalance);

    selfdestruct(owner);

}

}
```

Write a Solidity contract that defines a "Token" contract with the following functionality:
-The contract has a name, symbol, and total supply.
-The contract has a function that allows the owner to mint new tokens and add them to their balance.
-The contract has a function that allows a user to transfer tokens to another address.
-The contract has a function that returns the balance of a specific address.

```javascript
const Bank = artifacts.require("Bank");
contract("Bank", () => {
  it("should allow the owner to deposit, withdraw, transfer, and kill the contract", async () => {
    const bank = await Bank.new();
    const owner = await bank.owner();
    const recipient = "0x1234567890abcdef1234567890abcdef12345678";
    // Deposit 1 ether
    await web3.eth.sendTransaction({
      to: bank.address,
      from: owner,
      value: web3.utils.toWei("1", "ether")
    });
    assert.equal((await bank.balances(owner)).toString(), web3.utils.toWei("1", "ether"));
    assert.equal((await bank.totalBalance()).toString(), web3.utils.toWei("1", "ether"));
    // Withdraw 0.5 ether
    await bank.withdraw(web3.utils.toWei("0.5", "ether"), { from: owner });
    assert.equal((await bank.balances(owner)).toString(), web3.utils.toWei("0.5", "ether"));
    assert.equal((await bank.totalBalance()).toString(), web3.utils.toWei("0.5", "ether"));
    // Transfer 0.25 ether
    await bank.transfer(recipient, web3.utils.toWei("0.25", "ether"), { from: owner });
    assert.equal((await bank.balances(owner)).toString(), web3.utils.toWei("0.25", "ether"));
    assert.equal((await bank.balances(recipient)).toString(), web3.utils.toWei("0.25", "ether"));
    assert.equal((await bank.totalBalance()).toString(), web3.utils.toWei("0.5", "ether"));
    // Kill the contract
    await bank.kill({ from: owner });
    assert.equal(await web3.eth.getBalance(bank.address), 0);
  });
});
```

THANK YOU

Thank you again for choosing "Learn Truffle". I hope it helps you in your journey to learn Truffle and achieve your goals. Please take a small portion of your time and share this with your friends and family and write a review for this book. I hope your programming journey does not end here. If you are interested, check out other books that I have or find more coding challenges at: https://codeofcode.org